CHARL

Mars has an astoun
Colossal volcanoes,
Mount Everest, stretc
the northern hemisph
valley, thousands of
length, slices throug
to east ; vast open de
featureless, cover gre
After thousands of ye
the features of this re
are now, for the first t
for us a visible shape

So this atlas is unique
has man recorded wit
the physical features,
The extraordinary ac
atlas is to show, to w
metres, the position
each other of the cr
valleys and hills of
which, at its closest
less than 56,000,00

Text and illustrations
maps to form a com
picture of the Martia
which must come n
exploratory journey
end of this century,
foot on the terrain w
this book, and illustr
photographs from th
craft. Here and now
close and informed
new world they w

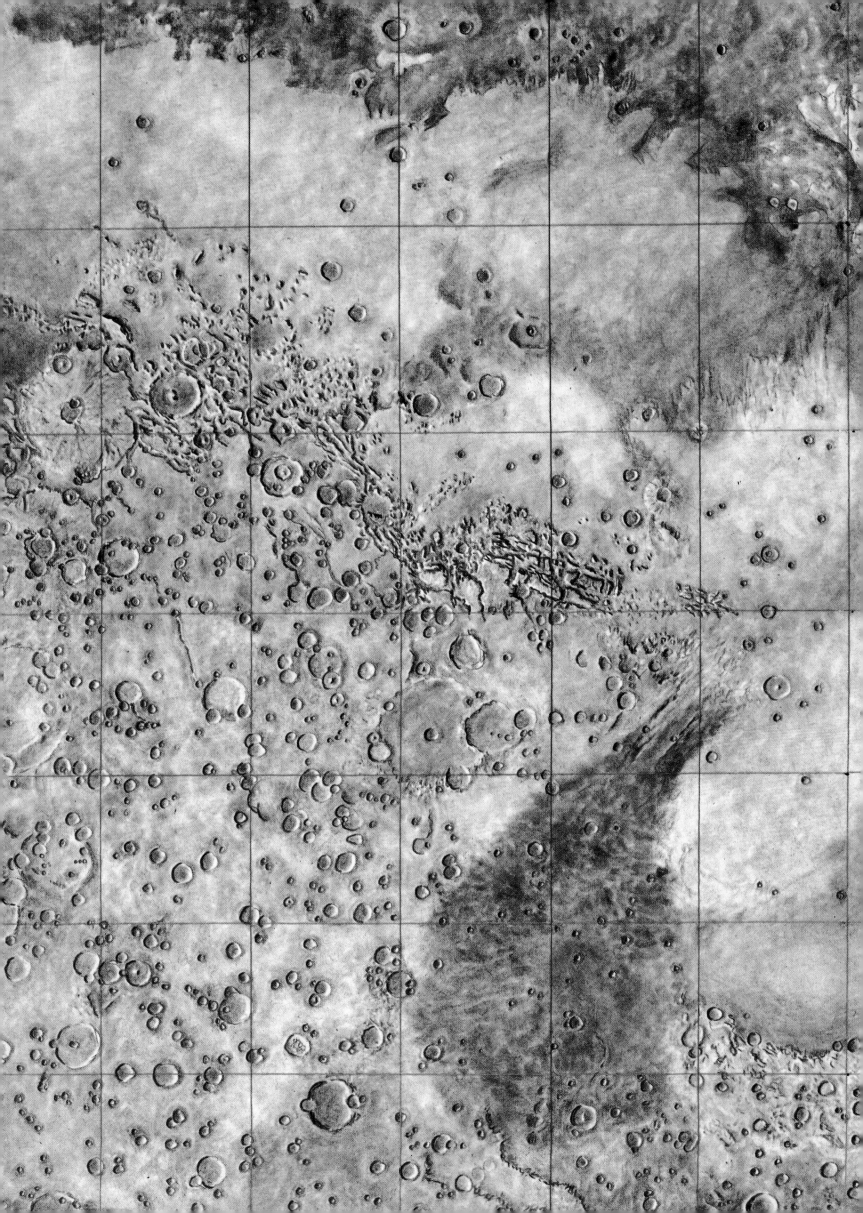

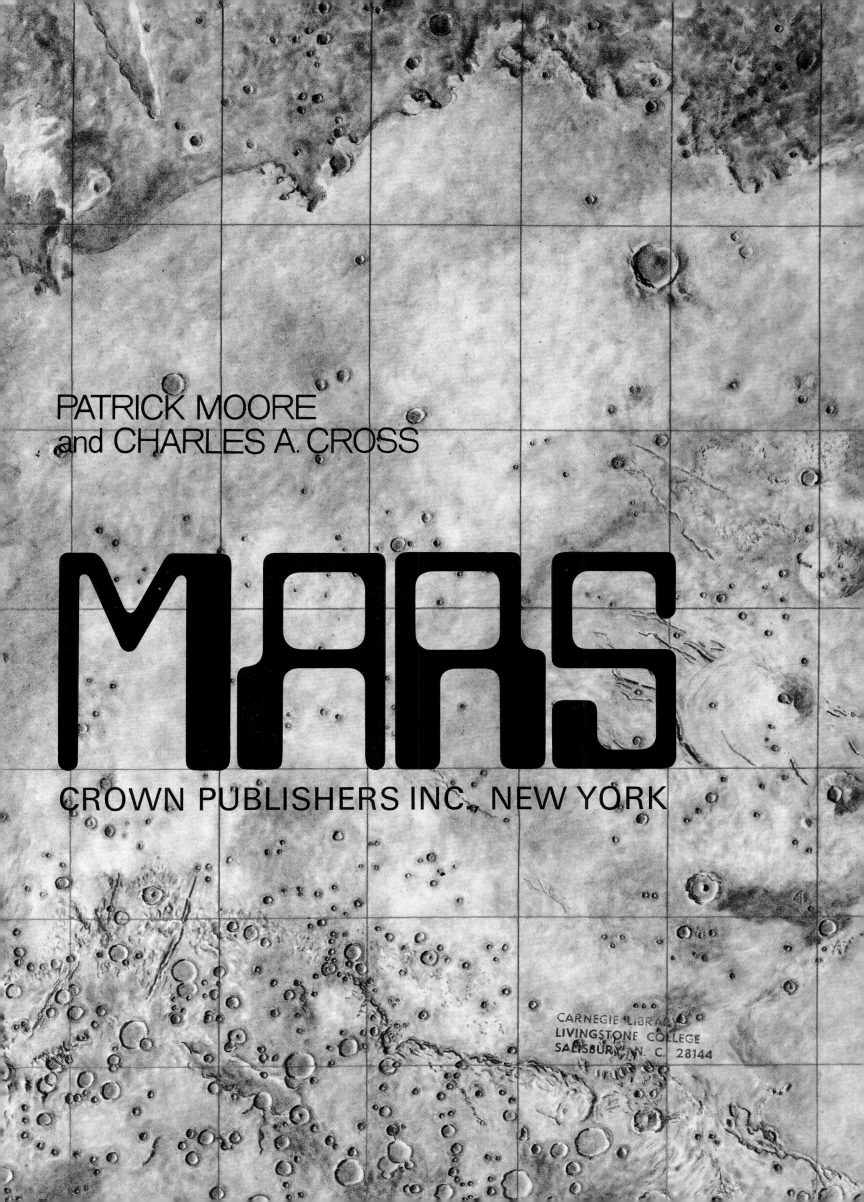

PATRICK MOORE
and CHARLES A. CROSS

MARS

CROWN PUBLISHERS INC., NEW YORK

CONTENTS

First published in the U.S.A. in 1973 by Crown Publishers Inc.

Library of Congress Catalog Card Number 73–78847

ISBN 0 517 50527 4

Designed by Nicholas Maddren. Edited by Ian Grant. Diagrams by Colin Rose. Cover illustration by Chris Foss.

Printed in the Netherlands

INTRODUCTION

In 1965, Mariner 4, a United States spacecraft, flew past Mars and sent back the first spectacular pictures, showing that there are craters there. Mariners 6 and 7 followed in 1969, and then, in 1971–2, the orbiting spacecraft Mariner 9 sent back thousands of amazingly detailed pictures. Two Russian spacecraft have also been put into orbits around Mars, and have obtained much further information. The result of their achievements is that it is now possible to construct charts of Mars which give us a real insight into the nature of the planet.

The charts in this book represent pioneering work. For the first time it is possible to present an atlas of Mars which is comparable with atlases drawn from the Moon (and, for that matter, for the Earth). Nobody has ever before been able to study the huge Martian volcanoes, the craters, and the incredible rift valleys. The maps are far more detailed than any previously drawn, and they lead us on to new and startling conclusions: whether or not Mars is sterile, it is by no means tectonically inactive, so that it cannot be classed as a dead world, like the Moon.

The globe of Mars has been divided into charts showing the four quadrants and the two poles. The charts were prepared from over 1500 individual Mariner 9 pictures, assembled into 30 mosaics by the United States Geological Survey's scientists for the Jet Propulsion Laboratory in California. These mosaics are accurate to within 60 km, and in this atlas any errors and inconsistencies have been reduced by incorporating the calculations of Merton E. Davies of the Rand Corporation of America. Over most of the globe the size of the smallest crater shown is 20 km in diameter at the equator and 10 km at latitude 60°, but over parts of the northern hemisphere the Mariner pictures may not have reached this degree of detail because of persistent haze. Because the computer-enhanced Mariner pictures show only the boundaries of changes in surface albedo, the depiction of the light and dark areas has been supplemented by information from Earth based maps of Mars.

For the charts in this atlas we have chosen the Conformal projections, which preserve undistorted on the map the shapes of features on the globe, and the directions between them, which means that circular craters, for instance, remain circular. However, this means sacrificing uniformity of scale. The surface between latitudes 60°N and 60°S is shown on Mercator projections, in which the scale increases with latitude, and is doubled at 60° from the equator. For polar regions the Polar Stereographic projection has been used. The scale increases with distance from the pole, and is doubled at the equator.

The charts have been drawn entirely by C. A. Cross, while the text has been written jointly by both authors. Our most grateful thanks are due to NASA and the JPL, who have kindly and readily given us co-operation in the work; special thanks are due to Merton E. Davies. Finally, we must express our thanks to the publishers, in particular to Nicholas Maddren and Ian Grant.

C. A. Cross
Patrick Moore.

Mariner 9 Launched towards Mars by an Atlas-Centaur rocket on 30 May 1971.

MARS IN THE SOLAR SYSTEM

Mars, the Red Planet, is one of the most fascinating of our neighbours in space. Venus is closer to Earth, but recent discoveries of the extremely high temperature and pressure on its surface have shown that it is likely to be much less hospitable than Mars. Mars is more like the Earth than any other planet, and, given the present state of our knowledge, it can be regarded as the one world in the Solar System where we may just possibly find traces of organic life.

Mars has been recognised from very early times, and, indeed, it cannot be overlooked. At its brightest it is more brilliant than any object in the sky apart from the Sun, the Moon and Venus, and it can always be identified by its striking red colour. It was this hue which led the ancients to name it after Ares or Mars, the mythological god of war.

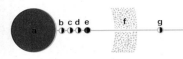

a Sun   d Earth   g Jupiter   j Neptune
b Mercury e Mars   h Saturn   k Pluto
c Venus   f Asteroids   i Uranus

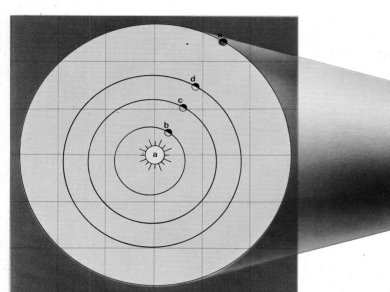

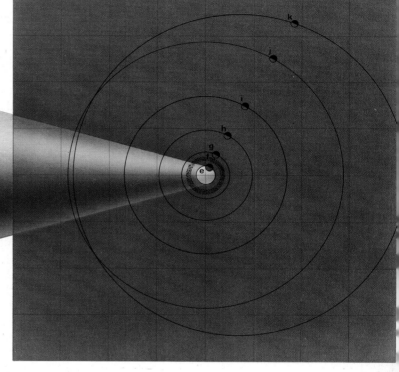

The Solar System *top* Relative mean distances of the planets from the Sun. Mars is about 225,000,000 km distant.

Orbits of the Planets *above* Left: the four inner planets. Right: Mars again, the asteroids, and the outer planets.

The Solar System is divided into two main parts. There is an inner group of planets, made up of Mercury, Venus, the Earth and Mars; then comes a wide gap, in which move many thousands of minor planets or asteroids; and beyond we come to the giants – Jupiter, Saturn, Uranus and Neptune. Pluto, which can at times recede far beyond the orbit of Neptune, also belongs to the outer group, even though its exact status is uncertain: it may be a true planet, or it may be nothing more than a former satellite of Neptune.

Mars moves around the Sun at a mean distance of 229,700,000 km, but its orbit is much less circular than that of the Earth, so that there is a greater range between its distance from the Sun at perihelion (when closest to the Sun, at 207,000,000 km) and at aphelion (farthest from the Sun, at 243,000,000 km). On Mars, summer occurs in the southern hemisphere when the planet is near perihelion, and so the southern summers are shorter and hotter than those in the northern hemisphere of the planet, while the winters are longer and colder. The seasons on Earth are similar, but the effects are much less noticeable, because the orbit of the Earth is very nearly circular.

Comparative Diameters *left* The Solar System consists of the five so-called terrestrial planets – Mercury, Venus, Earth, Mars and the distant Pluto – and the four giants – Jupiter, Saturn, Uranus and Neptune. The planets are drawn to scale: Mars, fourth from the top, is 6790 km in diameter; Jupiter, the largest, is 141,920 km in diameter.

The Orbits of Mars and Earth

In the Solar System, the orbit of Mars lies outside that of the Earth. The farther away from the Sun, the more slowly a planet travels: the average orbital velocity of Mars is only 24 km per second, as against 29·8 km per second for the Earth. Its revolution period or 'year' is 687 Earth days. It seems to move comparatively quickly against the starry background, and it was by studying the movements of Mars that the great astronomer Kepler, in the early 17th century, was able to draw up his Laws of Planetary Motion.

Mars is said to be at opposition when, seen from the Earth, it is directly opposite in the sky to the Sun (that is, when the Sun, Earth and Mars form a straight line). On average, oppositions occur every 780 days, or every alternate year. The most favourable oppositions occur when Mars is at or near perihelion, since it is then at its closest to the Earth, as was the case in 1971. Perihelic oppositions occur at intervals of about sixteen years. When well away from opposition Mars shines as a star of about the second magnitude, approximately equal to Polaris. At these times it is easily confused with a true star, though its red colour is always pronounced.

The Planet Mars *right* Despite difficulty, excellent pictures of Mars have been obtained. This photograph was taken at the Lowell Observatory, Flagstaff, Arizona. It shows the white polar cap, believed to be a mixture of solid carbon dioxide and ordinary ice; the dark regions, once thought to be due to organic material; and the red 'deserts'.

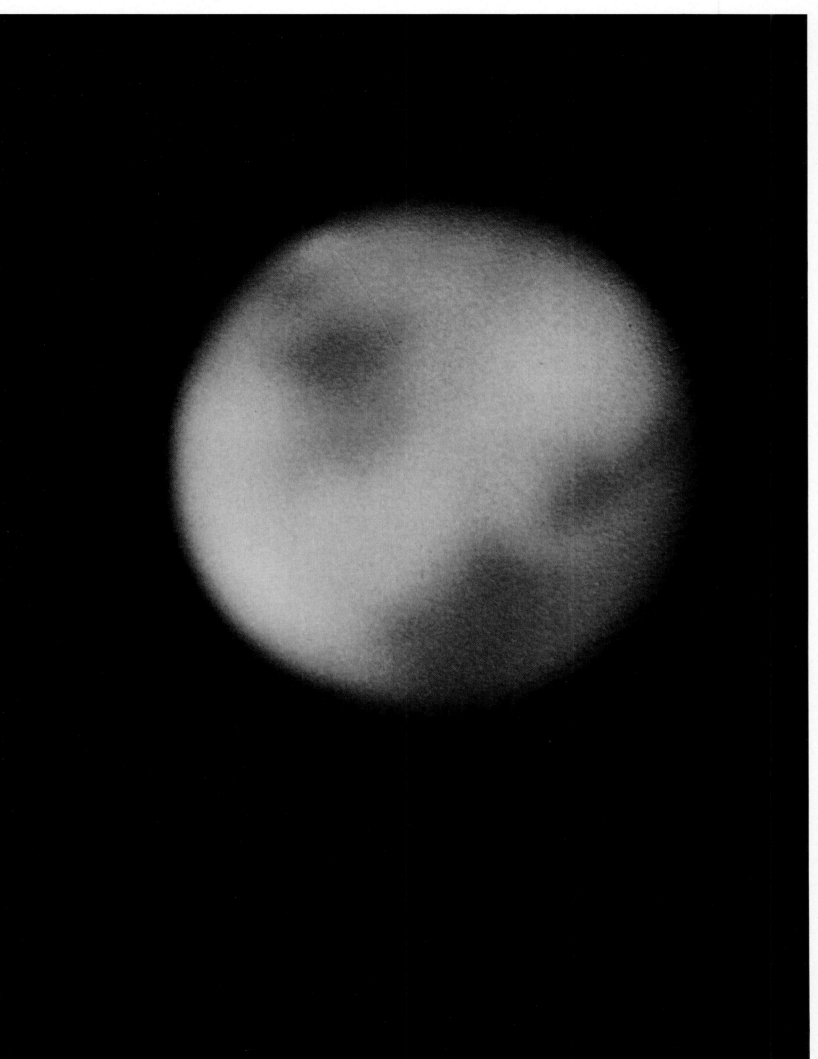

MARS AS A WORLD

In some ways Mars is not unlike the Earth. The main difference is that Mars is much smaller and less massive. Its diameter is only 6790 km, so that in size it is intermediate between the Earth and the Moon; its mass is 0·1 that of the Earth, and its escape velocity is 5 km per second (that is, any object leaving the surface of Mars at a velocity greater than 5 km per second would not be retained by the Martian gravitational field, and would escape into space). Because of this low mass, Mars has retained only a thin atmosphere, and there is no chance that human beings or advanced creatures of any type known to man could breathe there. However, it must be the next target for manned space flight.

Mars and Earth compared *left* Mars is much smaller than Earth: its diameter is a little over half that of our world. The surface area is 0·28 that of Earth.

Internal Constitution of Mars

As yet we know nothing definite about the internal constitution of Mars, and until the first soft-landing spacecraft send back seismic information from the surface we can do no more than speculate. The mean density of the planet is less than that of the Earth; the specific gravity is only 3·9 – in other words, Mars weighs 3·9 times as much as an equal volume of water would do. The specific gravity of the Earth is 5·5. Since a planet becomes less dense from its core towards its outer layers, this means that the mean density of Mars is about the same as that of the outer layers of the Earth.

It is doubtful whether Mars has a fluid core like the Earth's. Strong planetary magnetic fields are generated by dynamo effects in such a core, but the Russian measurements show that Mars has only a rather weak field. Although the question must remain open, surface evidence of tectonic activity perhaps favours the existence of such a core.

Appearance of Mars

Through a telescope, Mars is an intriguing sight. There are darkish areas, reddish-ochre tracts, and white caps covering the planet's poles. Early observers believed that the dark areas were seas and the red regions were land, but for almost a century now it has been realised that there can be no oceans on Mars. In fact, water cannot exist as a liquid on Mars, except at the very lowest areas of the surface, such as the great bowl of Hellas, where the atmospheric pressure is great enough for liquid water to form. A little water vapour has been detected in the atmosphere, and the existence of extensive permafrost has been suggested, although there is considerable doubt as to the amount of water locked up at the poles in the form of snow or ice. The visible surface of the white caps is certainly carbon dioxide snow, but under this, water ice exists.

It is tempting to suggest that the ochre tracts are deserts, and recent research indicates that this may be a

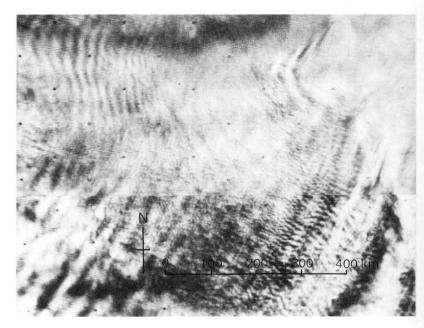

Clouds Over Mare Acidalium *above* This photograph, taken in March 1972, shows clouds over the Mare Acidalium, the largest dark feature in the north of Mars. At this time, winter in the northern hemisphere, most of the areas north of latitude +45° were cloud-covered; the flow of air over the surface features produces wave-clouds.

good name for them. Information from the orbiting Soviet spacecraft Mars 3 suggests that they are siliceous – that is they contain, or consist of, silica. However, they are cold by terrestrial standards. On Mars, at noon on the equator in midsummer, the temperature may rise to over 12°C, but at night a thermometer would show more than 70°C below zero.

The Atmosphere of Mars

Mars has an appreciable atmosphere. Until the beginning of this century it was thought that this atmosphere might even be comparable with that of the Earth, in which case Mars would have been able to support life of an advanced type. However, spectroscopic work carried out in the first part of the 20th century showed that the atmosphere is tenuous. In 1956 an analysis published by the French astronomer G. de Vaucouleurs gave a ground pressure of 85 millibars; it was believed that the main constituent must be nitrogen, with smaller amounts of carbon dioxide and water vapour. Had this been so, the Martian atmosphere would have been as dense as the Earth's

Structure of the Martian Atmosphere *left* The pressure is very low – about 5 millibars at the mean ground level. The temperature drops as the altitude increases, except for a rise in the ionosphere. During the 1971 dust storm the temperature was appreciably greater in the lower atmospheric levels.

Temperature in °C

Height in kilometres

Ionosphere — Peak Ion Density

Normal Temperature Profile

Stratosphere

Profile during dust storm

Haze layers

Troposphere

Nordus Gordii

Hellas

Pressure in millibars

(after W. K. Hartmann)

air at a height of about 16,000 metres above sea level. Although it would have been unbreathable, it would have acted as an effective screen against harmful radiations from space as well as from micro-meteorites. However, recent results have shown that the actual density is very much less than this.

The first really reliable measurements were made in 1965, from the American spacecraft Mariner 4. In the 'occultation experiment', the probe passed behind the planet; just before it was occulted by (or disappeared behind) the globe, the signals from it came to us after having passed through the Martian atmosphere, and the effects upon the signals showed clearly that all previous ideas had been wrong. Similar occultation experiments were carried out with the spacecraft of 1969 and 1971–2, and the results have been in good agreement.

Structure of the Atmosphere

The diagram on the opposite page shows the suggested structure of the Martian atmosphere, based on information available at present. The ground pressure is very low – in some places only 3 millibars, and nowhere more than 10 millibars: pressures which correspond to those in the Earth's stratosphere. At 20 km above the mean ground level, the pressure is down to 1 millibar. The Martian troposphere is assumed to end at about 30 km, and the centre of the ionosphere is at 140 km. The temperature gradient is of the same basic nature as that of the Earth's atmosphere, with a 'high temperature' zone in the ionosphere, though it must be remembered that this does not indicate any appreci-

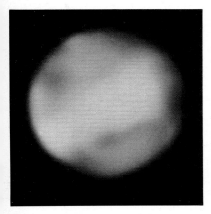

Cloud over Syrtis Major *above* The northern border of the Syrtis Major, to the far right of the disk, is obscured by a blue cloud. Photo: Capen, 3 April 1969.

able heat (in such measurements temperature is defined by the velocities of the atoms and molecules). The main constituent is carbon dioxide, and there are only traces of other gases. Water vapour is present only in extremely small amounts.

Atmospheric Pressure

The pressure is no greater than that of the Earth's air at more than 50,000 metres above sea level. In comparison with the Earth, and for the purposes of human survival, the Martian atmosphere is negligible. According to results from the Russian spacecraft, at an altitude of over 300 km the main constituent of the atmosphere is atomic hydrogen, and, curiously, it seems that the upper atmosphere may be more like that of Venus than that of the Earth. These results agree with measurements made of the amount of carbon dioxide above different regions of Mars, also carried out from the Mariner vehicles.

The Clouds of Mars

In general, the atmosphere of Mars is transparent. Dense clouds like those on Earth would not be expected in a tenuous carbon-dioxide atmosphere, and under normal conditions the surface features can be seen clearly, without obscuration. However, clouds do occur, and are of two main types (telescopic observations have been confirmed by data from Mariner 9). The so-called 'white clouds' lie at a high altitude and are not uncommon. It has been suggested that they are made up of ice or solid carbon dioxide crystals. They are especially pronounced at Martian sunrise and sunset. These clouds are distinct from what is often called the 'violet layer' or 'blue haze'. This is a haze in the Martian atmosphere which is virtually permanent. It cannot be seen through a telescope, but it reflects light of short wavelength (the blue end of the spectrum) and shows up when Mars is photographed in blue light. Photography in other lights enables observers to see features on Mars that may be obscured by this haze, since orange, yellow or red light penetrates it. Occasionally, the haze clears in patches, allowing the surface of Mars to be photographed in blue light as well, giving results of finer detail. The 'yellow clouds' are quite different. They seem to occur at low levels in the atmosphere, and are generally interpreted to be clouds of dust. During some oppositions of the planet major dust storms have been observed; typical cases were the storms of 1909, 1924, 1937, 1956 and 1971 (all of which were perihelic oppositions). They are discussed fully on page 17.

If the Martian atmosphere is so tenuous and, except during the major obscurations, so clear, it is likely that the surface of the planet is exposed to all kinds of radiations coming from space. The Earth is protected by its dense atmosphere, but the Martian atmosphere is useful only as a screen against micro-meteorites. This must have profound effects upon our ideas about life there.

Life on Mars

Intelligent life can be ruled out at once. The conditions are hopelessly unsuitable in every way. Plants, however, are much more adaptable, and can survive in the most unlikely places; there are some terrestrial organisms which do not even need oxygen. If we are to find any form of Martian life, it must necessarily be lowly; even an advanced plant, such as a flower, would be unable to exist in so hostile an environment. It used to be thought that the dark areas were due to organic matter, but the weight of present evidence is very much against anything of the sort.

On the other hand, it seems that Mars is not geologically inert, and the features shown by Mariner 9 indicate that much more atmosphere and water existed in the past than is the case now. If life could develop during the periods when conditions are less rigorous, it might possibly persist – particularly if, as is widely thought, the less rigorous periods recur at intervals of 25,000 years or so. Neither can we entirely discount some form of life underneath the surface, where it would be better protected from harmful radiation.

Occultation Experiment *right* As the spacecraft passes behind the planet, instead of transmitting direct to Earth (A and F), the Martian atmosphere causes fading in the radio signal, (from B to C, and D to E). These changes make it possible to measure pressure and temperature in the atmosphere.

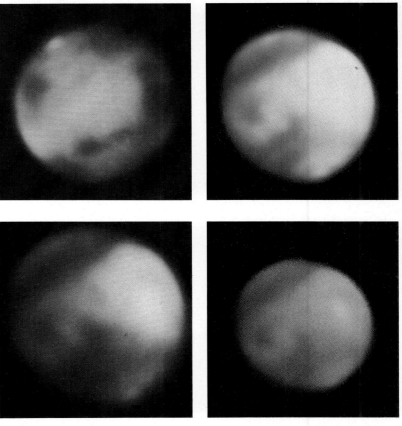

Cloud Photography *above* The four views show Mars taken in light of varying colours. At top left is a view which emphasises the area of cloud which forms every Martian summer over the Syrtis Major. The other three show the Syrtis Major to the left, covered by this cloud. In the centre is the Aethiopis region; the bright area to the right is Elysium. Photos: Capen, 1 April 1969, 20 May 1967.

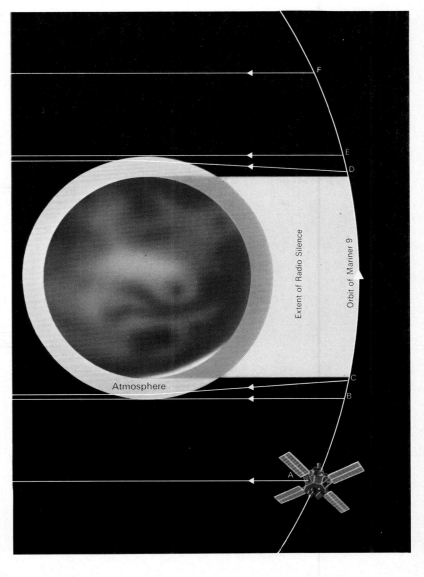

HISTORICAL EXPLORATION

Early telescopic observers of Mars believed that the planet was essentially similar to the Earth, despite its colder climate due to the greater distance from the Sun. The existence of an atmosphere was never in real doubt, and the white caps at the poles seemed to indicate that there was plenty of water locked up as ice and snow.

But the results of observation, during the 19th century, of the rate of decrease of the polar caps showed that the caps could not be more than a few centimetres deep, and analyses of the atmosphere showed that it is extremely thin. In 1877 Schiaparelli drew attention to the curious streaks which are still called 'canals'. Lowell claimed that these canals were artificial, and the argument raged for many decades. Only with the development of rocket probes has it been resolved.

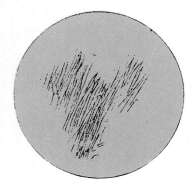

Huygens, 28 November 1659 This was the first sketch of Mars to show a recognisable feature. It was made with one of the small-aperture, long-focus refractors of the time, and it is greatly to Huygens' credit that he managed to see any markings at all. The triangular feature is easily identified as the Syrtis Major, the most conspicuous of all the dark areas on Mars – rather exaggerated in size.

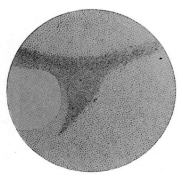

Schröter, 2 November 1800 Schröter was an enthusiastic and skilful observer of the Moon and planets, and his drawings of Mars were better than any previously made. The sketch given here again shows the Syrtis Major, comparatively accurately. Yet Schröter's interpretation was wrong; he believed the dark areas to be due to cloud phenomena in the atmosphere of Mars rather than true surface features.

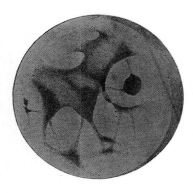

Schiaparelli, 26 December 1879 Here we see the famous canal network, first drawn in detail by Schiaparelli in 1877, from his 20 cm refractor at Milan. Again the Syrtis Major is identifiable, but the general aspect is quite different from that shown in the earlier drawings. At this period only Schiaparelli was recording canals; they were not described by other observers until seven years later.

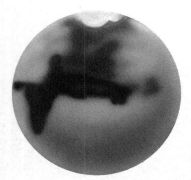

Antoniadi, early 20th century This is a typical view obtained with the great 83 cm refractor at the Meudon Observatory near Paris. Though he was using a very powerful telescope, Antoniadi recorded no linear canals, and had no belief in them. He made a long study of the planet, and his work provided a basis for all subsequent observational research. The Meudon refractor is ideally suited for planetary work, since a refractor always gives a particularly sharp and well defined image when used visually.

Moore, 16 August 1971 This sketch, made from the author's 31 cm reflector, is included to show a typical view of the planet as obtained with a telescope of moderate size. The Syrtis Major appears to the left, and the Sinus Meridiani (the zero for Martian longitudes) to the right. At this period the surface features were clear; the great dust storm did not begin until some weeks later.

Mars is a small planet, and can be well observed only for a few weeks to either side of opposition, so that telescopic workers have to make the most of their limited opportunities. Galileo, with his tiny telescope, failed to detect any surface features, though – rather surprisingly – he did note the phase. The first drawing of real value was made in 1659 by Christiaan Huygens. It shows a triangular patch which, although slightly large, is undoubtedly a representation of the Syrtis Major.

Following Huygens, more detailed observations were made at Paris by G. D. Cassini, who paid close attention to the polar caps and the seasonal effects. The rotation period was measured satisfactorily, and the existence of an atmosphere was established.

The next major advance was made by Sir William Herschel, best remembered for his discovery of the planet Uranus in 1781 and for his work on the distribution of stars in our Galaxy. Herschel regarded the reddish tracts as land, the dark regions as seas, and the polar caps as snow-fields – a point of view which seemed reasonable at the time. His contemporary Johann Schröter made some excellent drawings of Mars, though his interpretations were wrong; he believed the dark areas to be due to phenomena in the atmosphere.

The 19th Century
Improvements in telescopic equipment led to great advances during the 19th century. Two German observers, Beer and Mädler, compiled a reasonably good map, and from 1860 onward the features were carefully studied by many telescopic workers. Among these were Lockyer, Phillips, Proctor and Green, whose observations and drawings were of high accuracy.

The next stage in the story of Martian research began in 1877, when G. V. Schiaparelli, at Milan, drew an improved map and also showed strange, linear features which he called 'canali' or channels. He retained an open mind as to whether these channels were natural or artificial; but from 1895 onward Percival Lowell, who built the famous observatory at Flagstaff in Arizona mainly to observe Mars, strongly supported the idea that the features were true canals, of artificial origin. He believed that they made up a vast irrigation system, to distribute water from the melting polar caps, which shrank visibly during the Martian spring. Lowell remained convinced of the truth of this theory, but it was hotly challenged even in his lifetime (he died in 1916). His observations also were challenged; for instance E. M. Antoniadi, using the great 33 in refractor at Paris, maintained that 'nobody has ever seen a true canal', and that the linear features were due to optical illusions. Nowadays it seems that many of the canals have at least a basis of reality, as seen in many of the Mariner 9 photographs, though there can no longer be any doubt that they are natural features.

Drawing by Percival Lowell *below* In Lowell's sketches the canal network appears in its most highly developed state, and the general aspect is certainly artificial. However, few observers saw the canals in this form. The principal features of the surface are easily recognisable, but the whole drawing seems to be stylised. Lowell used the powerful refractor at his observatory at Flagstaff, but – significantly – he often stopped it down, so that the full aperture was not used.

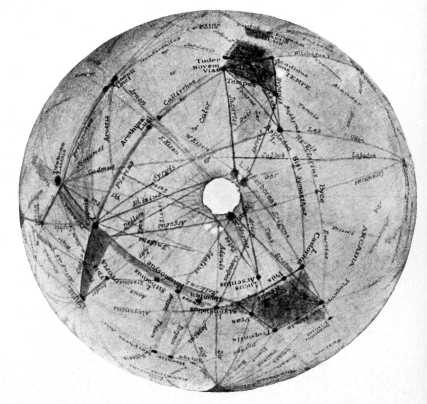

N. E. Green. Drawn by the English observer in 1877. Like all maps of the time, this has south to the top. Many of the familiar features are shown with considerable accuracy, as can be seen from a comparison with modern charts and photographs. The names, due mainly to R. A. Proctor, were in common use at the time. The Kaiser Sea (often nicknamed the Hourglass Sea) is the modern Syrtis Major, while Lockyer Land is Hellas, Herschel II Strait is Sinus Sabaeus, and so on. Already there were serious doubts as to whether the dark areas were sheets of open water, since astronomers had already found that the atmosphere is tenuous and that water must be scarce. No canals are shown on this chart, which was made just before Schiaparelli published his map.

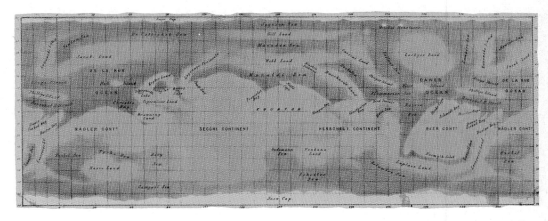

Giovanni Schiaparelli. Drawing made from observations between 1877 and 1886 with the 20 cm refractor at Milan. Despite the number of linear canals, this map was a decided improvement on any previous work, and most of the names we use today were introduced by Schiaparelli. We now know that the canals do not exist in the form in which Schiaparelli showed them, but — as Antoniadi pointed out in later years — some of them have a basis of reality, even though they are not in the least artificial in aspect. Schiaparelli's work began in 1877, and was more or less ended by his failing eyesight in 1890, though he made a few drawings at subsequent oppositions. He noted the seasonal changes associated with the polar caps, which he believed to be due to a layer of ice or snow.

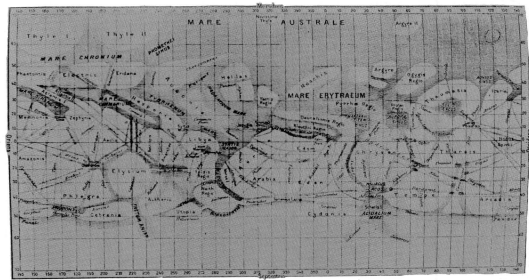

Percival Lowell. Drawn in 1905, this chart is typical of Lowell's work. He was convinced that the canals were artificial, and this certainly influenced his drawings, most of which were made with the Flagstaff refractor. The canals are even more stylized than as shown by Schiaparelli, and some of them are double; this was the phenomenon which Lowell called gemination (duplication) Schiaparelli's nomenclature is followed, though Lowell added some names on his own account. Lowell also regarded the so-called wave of darkening as very significant. He wrote that as a polar cap shrank in the Martian spring and early summer, the dark regions in high latitudes became more pronounced, with changes in colour His attitude was summed up in his book *Mars and its Canals*: 'That Mars is inhabited by beings of some sort or other we may consider as certain as it is uncertain what those beings may be'.

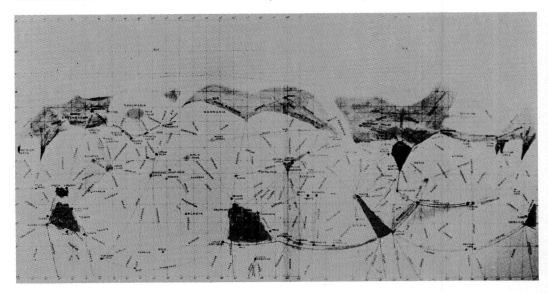

E. M. Antoniadi. Map compiled from Antoniadi's observations with the Meudon 83 cm refractor. The aspect is very different from that shown by Schiaparelli and Lowell. There are no linear canals, and Antoniadi stated categorically that nobody has ever seen a true canal on Mars. He respected Schiaparelli as an observer, but dismissed the artificial appearance of the features Lowell observed as due to optical illusion. Antoniadi revised the nomenclature of Mars yet again, though he retained most of Schiaparelli's names with only slight modifications. He was an expert observer, and had the advantage of using a very large telescope; it is therefore not surprising that his map of Mars was the best of its time, and was not surpassed until the 1950s, when Mars came under close study at many observatories. A comparison of his map with the Mariner results confirms that he was, in general, remarkably accurate.

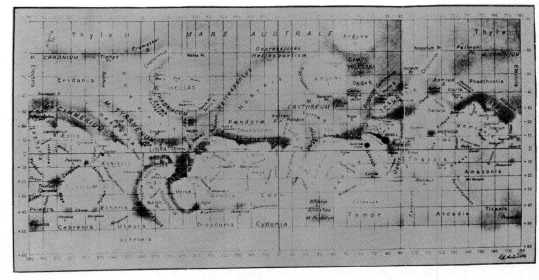

MODERN TELESCOPIC OBSERVATION

The modern phase of telescopic observation of Mars is generally taken to have begun in 1877 — not because of the rise to fame (or notoriety) of the canals, but because Schiaparelli's map was a definite improvement upon any previous work. Also, 1877 was the year of the introduction of the new nomenclature, replacing the older, romantic names.

The increase in size and quality of telescopes led to improved views of Mars. But the world's greatest instruments have seldom been used for planetary observation; really large telescopes are intended for studies of remote stars and star systems, and to use them for mapping Mars would not exploit their capabilities. Moreover, no photograph can ever show as much as can be seen by direct viewing with a moderate telescope.

Mars and the Earth move around the Sun in different periods, so Mars is well placed for observation for only a few months every alternate year. It is a comparatively small world, and when it is a long way from the Earth not even a giant telescope will show much upon its tiny red disk.

Because the Martian orbit is much more eccentric than ours, not all oppositions are equally favourable. When opposition occurs with the planet near perihelion, the minimum distance from Earth can be reduced to less than 56,000,000 km; this was the case in 1956 and again in 1971. (At perihelic oppositions, Mars is well south of the celestial equator, so that observers in Europe and the United States have to contend with an inconveniently low altitude above the horizon).

At its most brilliant, Mars can outshine every object in the sky apart from the Sun, the Moon and Venus, and this, combined with its strongly red colour, makes it truly striking. Its apparent diameter reaches 25·7 seconds of arc.

At aphelic oppositions, however, the distance always exceeds 96,000,000 km, and the apparent diameter is much smaller; in 1980, for instance, it will never attain 14 seconds of arc. This also means that the period of time during which observations can be made, to either side of the opposition date, is much less.

Table of Oppositions

Oppositions for the rest of the present decade will take place as follows:

1973 October 25.
Maximum apparent diameter: 21″·4.
Maximum magnitude: −2·1.
Mars will be on the borders of Pisces and Aries.

1975 December 15
Maximum apparent diameter: 16″·5.
Maximum magnitude: −1·4.
Mars will be in Taurus.

1978 January 22.
Maximum apparent diameter: 14″·3.
Maximum magnitude: −1·1.
Mars will be on the borders of Gemini and Cancer.

1980 February 25.
Maximum apparent diameter: 13″·8.
Maximum magnitude 1·0.
Mars will be in Leo.

The axial inclination of Mars is almost the same as that of the Earth (24·0°, as against 23·5°), so that the seasons are of the same general type, though of course they are much longer; the Martian year amounts to 687 Earth days. At perihelic oppositions, the Martian south pole is turned towards us, and so before spacecraft were able to photograph the planet the southern features were much better known than those in the northern part of the planet. Astronomical convention shows drawings and maps of Mars with south at the top (as in the telescopic view from the Earth's northern hemisphere). The NASA convention is to put north at the top, and

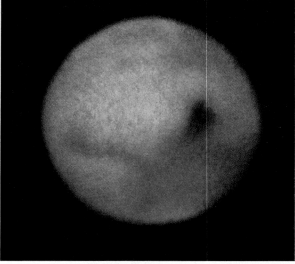

1. 29 May 1969. The northern cap is visible, with the Syrtis Major to the right of the disk (C. F. Capen, 131 cm reflector).

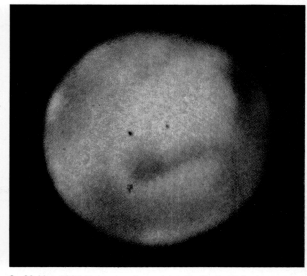

2. 29 May 1969. Taken two hours later, the Syrtis Major is now almost at the edge of the disk (C. F. Capen, 131 cm reflector).

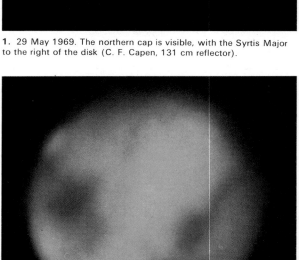

3. The Mare Acidalium is prominent near the top (north), and the Sinus Meridiani is near the central meridian (C. F. Capen, 131 cm reflector).

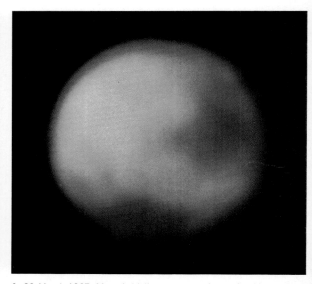

4. 29 March 1967. Mare Acidalium very prominent. A white cloud is easily visible to the upper left of the disk (C. F. Capen 131 cm reflector).

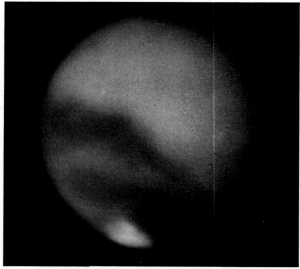

5. 17 August 1956. The south cap is prominent, and the Mare Sirenum is well placed (W. S. Finsen, 43 cm refractor).

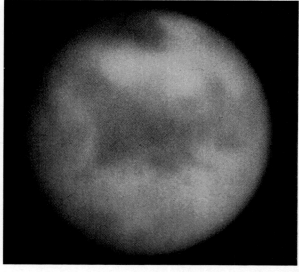

6. 29 August 1956. The Mare Acidalium appears to the upper left, and the south cap has virtually disappeared (W. S. Finsen, 43 cm refractor).

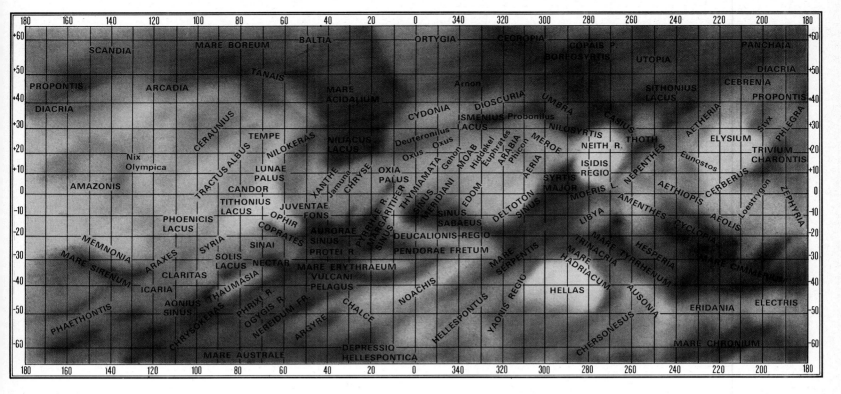

I.A.U. Map of Mars *above* This chart is a coloured interpretation of the official map approved by the International Astronomical Union. It is a Mercator projection, of the temperate and equatorial regions of Mars.

this procedure has been adopted in the present atlas.

The Rotation of Mars

Look at Mars through a moderately powerful telescope, under good conditions, and considerable detail will be visible. The polar cap will stand out, unless it is after midsummer in the hemisphere of Mars which is inclined towards us. The dark markings will be easy to see, and their characteristic outlines will be recognisable with a little practice.

The effects of the rotation of Mars are very evident. The apparent shift of a feature across the disk is obvious after a relatively short period of observation. Because the rotation period is approximately 40 minutes longer than ours, any

features will come to the central meridian 40 minutes later each day.

The map on this page has been compiled entirely from telescopic observations made from Earth, and shows all the prominent features. The nomenclature used is that accepted by the International Astronomical Union, and is based on that of Schiaparelli, with additions and alterations by Antoniadi and others. The features near the Martian poles cannot be shown on a Mercator projection.

The Dark Areas

Of the dark areas, much the most prominent is the Syrtis Major, which can be

Orbit of Mars *below* The drawing shows the orbits of Mars and the Earth, drawn to scale and with correct eccentricities; the Earth's orbit is practically circular, while that of Mars is decidedly eccentric. The last really favourable opposition was that of 1971, while the next will take place in 1986; oppositions in 1975, 1978, 1980 and 1982 will be unfavourable.

seen with a very small telescope when Mars is near opposition. It is shown in photographs 1 and 2, and cannot be mistaken. Extending from it (to the left, in 1 and 2) is the Sinus Sabaeus, a long darkish region, which in turn leads to the Sinus Meridiani or Meridian Bay, clearly shown in photographs 2 and 3. This was originally selected as the zero for Martian longitudes by J. H. Mädler, in the 1830s, so that it has been regarded as the 'Greenwich' for Mars. The modern zero is defined by the crater Airy-O, described on page 41.

The Mare Acidalium

The chief dark area in the northern hemisphere is the Mare Acidalium, best seen in photograph 4. Its characteristic wedge shape makes it stand out, and during aphelic oppositions, with the Martian north pole tilted toward us, it appears as the most prominent dark feature on the disk. It used to be thought that the dark areas were depressions (possibly sea beds) while the bright desert regions were elevated, but it is now known that there is little correlation between height and surface markings as they appear from Earth.

Hellas

South of the Syrtis Major is the famous circular plain Hellas, which may at times

appear so brilliantly white that it may be mistaken for an extra polar cap. Its aspect is variable: for instance it was strikingly bright during the 1969 opposition, much less so during 1971, even before the start of the dust storm. It appears in photograph 1. Formerly it was thought to be a high plateau which retained its snowy covering for a long time; we now know it to be a depression — in fact the deepest area on Mars, and the only place, as far as we know, where the atmospheric pressure is high enough for liquid water to exist. Mariner photographs show it to contain very few topographical features.

Prominent dark features in the Southern hemisphere include Mare Erythraeum, Aurorae Sinus and Mare Sirenum, of which the first two are well shown in photograph 3 and the third in photograph 4. In the northern hemisphere, in much the same longitude, is the Nix Olympica, which is not a difficult object to see through a telescope, under good conditions, but is not shown on the photographs given here — an indication that so far as planetary detail is concerned, the eye can still surpass the camera. We now know that Nix Olympica is a huge volcano; but from Earth its nature could never be discovered, since it appears only as a tiny patch.

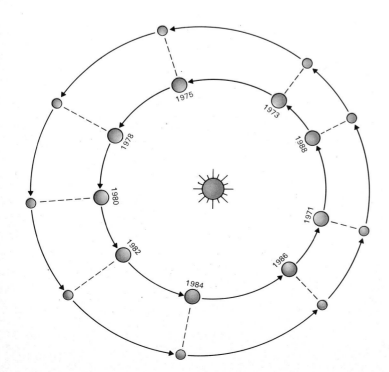

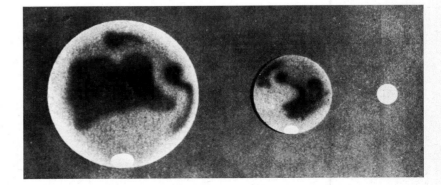

Apparent Size of Mars *above* At its nearest, at perihelic opposition, Mars can approach the Earth to within 56,000,000 km and its apparent diameter can then attain 25·7 seconds of arc. (It is best seen at this time from Earth's southern latitudes.) At its furthest, when at conjunction and at aphelion, it can recede to over 404,000,000 km, and show an apparent diameter of only 3·5 seconds of arc.

EXPLORATION BY SPACECRAFT

As long as Mars had to be studied only by telescopic observation from Earth, our knowledge was bound to remain limited. Even under excellent conditions, and using a large telescope, an observer can never see Mars better than he can see the Moon with the help of good binoculars. Photography is of limited help, and no photograph can record as much planetary detail as is actually visible with a moderate instrument. Also, spectroscopic analysis is very difficult to carry out through our own atmosphere, so that there was no really reliable information about the Martian atmospheric pressure and composition. Then, in the 1960s, it became possible to dispatch automatic probes to carry out studies from close range. Within a decade we had learned more about Mars than in the previous ten centuries.

The first attempt to send a probe to Mars was made by the Russians. On 1 November 1962 they sent up Mars 1, which entered the correct orbit, but when it reached 115,000,000 km from Earth radio contact with it was lost, and never regained.

The first successful vehicle was Mariner 4, launched on 28 November 1964. On 15 July 1965 it by-passed Mars at 9850 km, sending back the pictures which showed the surface of the planet to be scarred with craters. Mariner 4 also showed that the atmosphere is much less dense than had been previously thought. At about the same time the Russians had sent up Zond 2, which was launched on 30 November 1964. On 6 August 1965 it probably by-passed Mars at 1500 km, but well before then it also had gone out of radio contact, so that it must be regarded as a failure.

The next probes were Mariners 6 and 7, of 1969, which flew past the planet on 31 July and 5 August respectively. Mariner 6 studied the equatorial regions, while Mariner 7's coverage included the south pole. Each vehicle carried out improved studies of the atmosphere. The photographic coverage was much more extensive than with Mariner 4, and the pictures were far clearer. However, all these early spacecraft had to undertake their close-range research over a very short period of only a few hours; when they had passed Mars once they continued in perpetual orbits of the Sun, and did not return to the neighbourhood of the Red Planet.

Orbiting Spacecraft
A different principle was followed with the spacecraft of 1971—2, from which most of our reliable knowledge has been gained. The plan was to send the spacecraft to Mars and then put them

Launch of Mariner 9 *below* Launched, on 30 May 1971, by a massive Atlas-Centaur multi-stage rocket, the Mariner 9 craft was protected during its journey through the Earth's atmosphere in the cone of the rocket. After jettisoning the rocket only one other course change was needed throughout the journey.

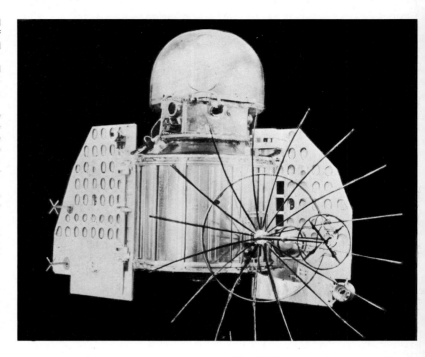

Mars 1 *above* This spacecraft was the first to be sent towards Mars. It was launched by the Russians on 1 November 1962, and apparently achieved the correct course. It was tracked out to about 115,000,000 km, a record at that time, but contact was then lost. It may have passed within 208,000 km of Mars.

into orbits round the planet, providing close-range coverage over a protracted period. There were four vehicles altogether, two Russian and two American. Of the Soviet spacecraft, Mars 2, sent up on 19 May 1971, reached the neighbourhood of Mars on 27 November, and was put into an elliptical, 18-hour orbit at an angle of 48·9° to the Martian equator. Its distance from the planet ranged between 40,000 and 2210 km. Just before entering orbit, it ejected a capsule which carried a Soviet emblem down onto the surface of Mars. The probe itself continued to function until well into 1972, and much valuable information was obtained from it.

The same was true of Mars 3, launched on 29 May 1971. By 2 December it had approached Mars, and released a descent capsule which made a parachute landing at latitude −45°, longitude 158°, between Phaethontis and Electris. Unfortunately, transmissions from the lander failed after only 20 seconds, so that nothing positive was learned from it. Subsequently Mars 3, like Mars 2, continued in orbit, and provided information about the Martian atmosphere and the surface texture.

Mariners 8 and 9
The Mariner 8 launch vehicle failed immediately after take off, and fell unceremoniously into the sea. This meant that the mission profile had to be modified so that Mariner 9 could undertake the entire research programme. It was launched on 30 May 1971. On 5 June a trajectory correction was made, and proved to be so accurate that no other corrections were necessary during the whole of the 167-day flight to Mars.

On 14 November, the spacecraft was inserted into Martian orbit by a 15-minute motor burn, and two days later, on the fourth revolution, a second 6-second firing made a further correction. Another trim manoeuvre was made on 30 December, changing the lowest altitude above Mars from 1387 to 1650 km. This is the final orbit for the probe. The inclination of the orbit to the Martian equator is 64·4° and the period is 11 hrs 58 mins. Already the orbit has provided new information about the shape and composition of Mars; for instance the original orbit was affected by an unexpected variation in the equatorial-plane gravity field.

The Mariner 9 Spacecraft
Mariner 9 is a complicated vehicle containing instruments of various kinds. The all-important cameras functioned excellently, and could be controlled from Earth — which is just as well, since when the probe reached the neighbourhood of Mars little of the surface could be seen, because of the great dust storm. Direct switching on and off of the equipment had its difficulties, because a radio signal takes several minutes to travel from Earth to Mars. Therefore the spacecraft carries a computer, whose programme could be amended by instructions from Earth and which then took over control of the equipment.

With a few minor exceptions, all the equipment in Mariner 9 worked excellently for almost a year after the probe had reached the neighbourhood of Mars. Finally, on 27 October 1972, as the ground controllers were preparing to manoeuvre the spacecraft, the supply of nitrogen on board ran out. Without being able to use the attitude control jets, the controllers could no longer aim the picture transmitting antenna toward the Earth, and so the mission was ended with a command turning off the transmitter. Between 13 November 1971 and the final failure of the nitrogen, Mariner had sent back 7329 photographs.

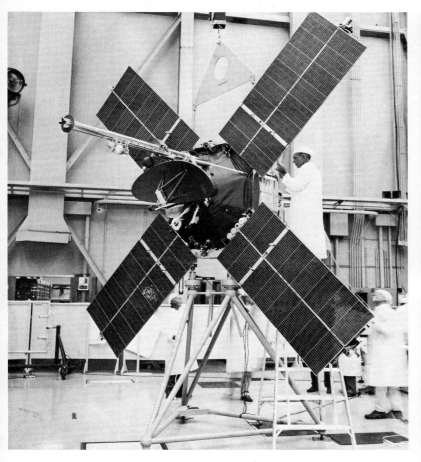

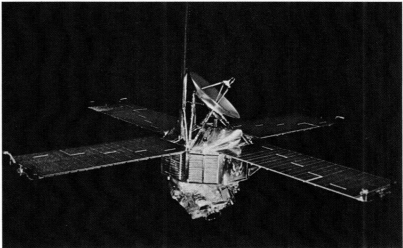

Mariner 4 *above* In the hangar at Cape Kennedy, the four solar panels, 2 metres long and 1 metre wide, are being attached. During the flight, these face towards the Sun, gathering energy. Small solar pressure vanes, acting as an auxiliary attitude control system, are located at the end of each panel.

Mars 3 *above right* This was the Russian spacecraft which deposited a landing capsule on the Martian surface. However, this particular experiment failed through a defect in the transmitting mechanism and the most important contributions from the probe were in connection with the Martian atmosphere.

Temperature measurements were reliably made; the infra-red radiometer sent back new data about the surface temperature, and results from the ultra-violet and infra-red spectrometers have confirmed that the atmosphere is made up principally of carbon dioxide.

To take Earth bacteria to Mars at the present stage would be a scientific tragedy, since subsequent investigations by Viking and its successors might not be able to distinguish between indigenous and imported life. The Russians have stated that the landing capsules from Mars 2 and 3 were fully sterilised,

which should be an effective precaution. Mariner 9 was not completely sterilised, but its biological contamination was minimised, and its orbit round Mars·was chosen so that it would not impact the planet for at least 50 years.

All in all, Mariner 9 was certainly the most successful of all planetary probes sent up during the first fifteen years of practical space research. It carried out not only its own scheduled programme, but also part of that of the luckless Mariner 8. Undoubtedly it surpassed the most optimistic hopes of those who planned and built it.

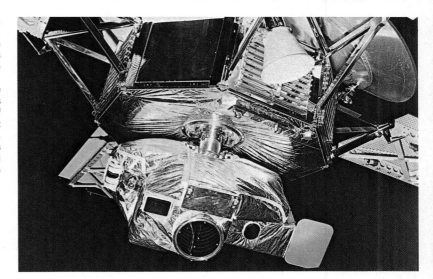

Journey of Mariner 9 The journey to Mars *below* lasted from May until November 1971. As Mariner 9 approached Mars it passed the two satellites *below right* and was put into an elliptical orbit around the planet.

Mariner 9 *above right* Similar to earlier American spacecraft, but with an added rocket motor. The cameras *right* formed the most important items of equipment. They were controlled by a computer on board, programmed from Earth.

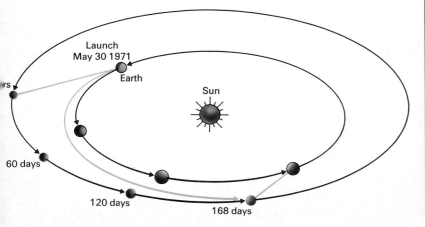

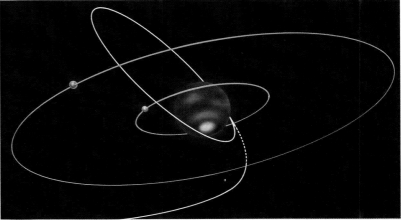

SURFACE VARIATIONS

Although the main features of Mars are permanent, there has never been any serious doubt that definite variations occur. These were noted more than a century and a half ago, and it was realised that Mars, unlike the Moon, is anything but an inert and changeless world.

The changes are of two main types: seasonal and irregular. The seasonal variations are bound up with the cycle of the polar caps, whereas the irregular variations take the form either of well marked changes of shape in certain of the dark areas (such as the Solis Lacus) or of the temporary extension of a dark region onto the adjacent desert. It was easy to account for these variations by the development, advance and subsequent retreat of vegetation; now, however, the possibility of vegetation appears slight.

1 May 22, 0210 hrs.

2 June 21, 0130 hrs.

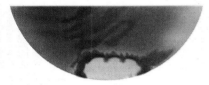

3 July 6, 0020 hrs.

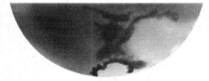

4 August 16, 2200 hrs.

5 September 28, 2015 hrs.

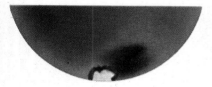

6 October 10, 1945 hrs.

Changes in the South Polar Cap
above Decrease of the south polar cap of Mars in 1972, from observations made by Patrick Moore with the 12½ in. reflector at his observatory at Selsey.

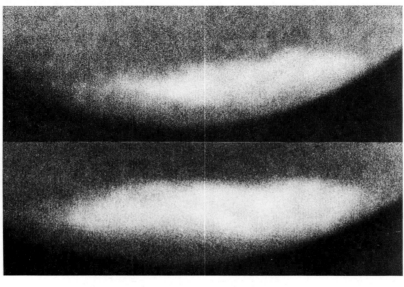

Composition of the Polar Caps
There is no doubt that the seasonal cycle of the Martian polar caps is of fundamental importance. At midwinter they are large and brilliant, covering wide areas; with the coming of warmer weather they shrink, until by Martian midsummer they appear very small. According to most authorities, the southern cap may disappear altogether, although its northern counterpart never completely vanishes. This is only to be expected in view of the greater extremes of temperature in the south.

When a cap is shrinking, it is often found that there is a dark band or collar around its periphery. This was first described in detail by Lowell, who attributed it to a temporary polar sea or marsh around the edge of the melting cap. Recent information seems to dispose of this attractive idea; it has even been suggested that the dark collar is due to nothing more than a contrast effect. Although it is not shown on the Mariner 7 photographs, Mariner 9 does

The 'Wave of Darkening' *below* This diagram is based on observations made by G. de Vaucouleurs at the Péridier Observatory in 1939. It shows the development and propagation of the seasonal dark flow between Hellas and Noachis. 1: May 27; 2: July 3; 3: August 9. De Vaucouleurs measured the rate of flow as 20 km per day.

show a dark band around the remnants of the north polar cap.

It may also be misleading to say that a polar cap melts in the Martian spring. The material may sublime – that is, change directly from the solid into the gaseous state without liquefaction. Lowell, of course, believed caps to be due to ice or snow. It now seems much more likely that solid carbon dioxide is the main constituent, though an admixture of ordinary ice must be present as well.

Even in Lowell's day it was known that a water ice cap would have to be very thin; otherwise the relatively weak solar radiation would be unable to disperse it. Even if this were possible, dispersal of a thick cap would release a vast amount of water vapour into the atmosphere, since at maximum extent it covers a very wide area, and it shrinks quickly after the end of winter. In many ways a carbon dioxide cap seems more plausible from a purely observational point of view, but we must also take into account the 'wave of darkening' effect.

The 'Wave of Darkening'
According to G. de Vaucouleurs and others, the shrinking of the polar cap has a marked effect upon the development of the dark areas. It is said that as the cap decreases, the nearby dark areas become more definite and more intense. The effect takes the form of a

The South Polar Cap of Mars *left* This pole, shown on the map on page 42, is seen in far-encounter photographs by Mariner 6 in 1969. Considerable detail is shown, and the shape of the cap is well marked, but there is no indication of the peripheral dark collar so often reported by Earth-based observers.

wave of darkening, starting in high latitudes and sweeping steadily down toward the equator.

This used to be easy to explain; the icy cap, in melting, would release water vapour, and this would be wafted down into the temperate and equatorial regions, so that the vegetation would start to develop. Yet if the caps are largely solid carbon dioxide, and the dark regions are not organic, the effect is much less easy to understand. There have even been serious doubts about the reality of the effect, and some observers (including the present writers) are dubious about it. Though variations in intensity of many of the dark regions are certainly real, a virtually regular wave of darkening is a different matter.

The same is true of the irregular variations. The Solis Lacus, shown on the map on page 35, varies obviously in form from one opposition to the next, and there have been cases of extensive, temporary spreading of dark regions on to adjacent deserts. If there is no organic covering of parts of the surface an explanation is very difficult.

New Topographical Information
Another puzzle in connection with the seasonal cycle of the polar caps is that we no longer believe the dark areas to be depressions and the bright areas elevations. Ironically, Hellas (once regarded as a plateau) is now known to be a deep depression, while the so-called Depressio Hellespontica is much loftier. Many observers have reported a seasonal 'dark flow' from a polar cap along what were taken to be depressed areas – for instance, between Noachis and Hellas; but this whole concept must now be drastically revised. All we can say with certainty is that a seasonal cycle does occur, and is intimately bound up with the more or less regular increase and decrease of the two polar caps.

The drawings on the far left of this page are based on observations by Patrick Moore in 1971, and show the seasonal decrease of the southern polar cap. (Since this was a perihelic opposition, the southern hemisphere of Mars was tilted toward the Sun and the Earth.) Early in the opposition – when Mars drew close enough to be properly observed – the southern cap was very extensive, covering regions such as Mare Australe and Thyle, and extending down almost to the Syrtis Major. By late May it had decreased somewhat, but was still very large. By late June it had decreased considerably, and there was a prominent dark collar, (possibly due to contrast effects). The shrinkage continued through July, with the uncovering of regions such as the Mare Australe and the persistence of the peripheral collar. During August the boundary of the cap became irregular, as usually happens at this stage of the cycle, while the dark collar was much

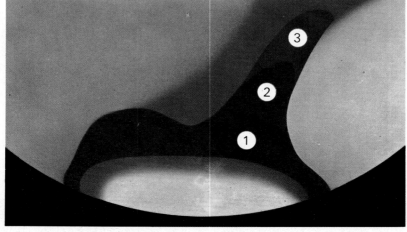

November   January   March

15 km · 10 · 5 · 0 · −5

less in evidence. This trend continued
in September, and by mid-October the
cap — now devoid of a peripheral collar —
had become so small that it was not
easy to see at all. Later developments
were obscured by the onset of the major
dust storm which covered almost all of
Mars between October and the end of
the year, during the time when Mariner 9
and Mars 2 and 3 reached the neighbourhood of the planet.

The 'Yellow Clouds'

Clouds on Mars are of two main types.
The high altitude clouds, described on
page 9, are scattered and of small extent. The so-called 'yellow clouds' are
entirely different and may at times cover
vast areas of the planet. There were
major obscurations in 1971, 1956 and
1924, for instance; others occurred in
1911 and 1909.

There is no suggestion that the obscurations are due to clouds of a terrestrial type, and they are usually attributed
to dust or sand storms. They may
develop quite quickly, and persist for
several weeks or even months, so that
the disk of the planet appears more or
less featureless. This was the case in
late 1971, from early October through to
the end of the year, so that when
Mariner 9 first went into orbit round
Mars the programme of photographing
the surface had to be postponed.

From Earth it is difficult to learn much
about the height of the dust layer, but
reliable information has come from
Mariner 9. It seems that in 1971 the
dust extended almost to the top of Nix
Olympica and Nodus Gordii, the highest
known points on Mars, which attain
an altitude of over 20 km. The obscuring
effect is virtually total, and as the
affected areas are extensive there must
be a considerable amount of dust or
sand in the atmosphere during a major
storm. The problem is: how can it get
there?

Martian Winds

The obvious explanation is that material
is whipped up from the ochre-coloured
areas by Martian winds. Probably the
wind velocities are high, and it is true
that fine material can hang in even a
tenuous atmosphere for long periods.
There is the terrestrial case of the
Krakatoa eruption in 1883, when dust
sent into the upper air remained there
for two years. On the other hand, it has
been suggested that since a wind in the
thin Martian atmosphere would have
little force (whatever might be its
velocity), it is rather difficult to see how
so much dust could be whipped up in
so short a time.

The most obscuring storms of the
present century seem to have taken place
at or near the time of perihelic oppositions (1971 being the most recent case),
and this has led to a suggestion that the
dust may be due to active vulcanism.
If the Martian volcanoes were capable
of erupting strongly enough, and spreading material around the upper atmosphere, the quick development and the
persistence of the storms would be
easier to explain; but this is a minority
view and Mariner 9 showed no indication of continuing vulcanism in 1972,
when the dust had cleared away and
the features had again become visible.

While a major storm is in progress,
much of the planet may be covered, as
in late 1971. This dust must subsequently settle, and after the end of the
storm the dark features such as the
Syrtis Major reappear, apparently un-
altered. Yet if the dust settled over them,
one might expect that they would be at
least less conspicuous than before the
onset of the storm; and if storms were
comparatively frequent, it would be

reasonable to suppose that the whole
planet would be overlaid with a layer of
uniform, ochre-coloured material. But,
from the observed behaviour of these
regions, this is not the case.

It was generally thought that the
dark regions must be organic, so that the
vegetation could push aside the dust
which settled upon it; this was one of the
main arguments for believing that some
sort of life must exist on Mars. On

present evidence such a theory is untenable. But it is unlikely that the dust
would settle in preferential areas after a
storm. We need to know more about the
force of the winds, but as yet we have
only a very elementary knowledge of
the wind circulation system on Mars.

In a way, it was fortunate that
Mariner 9 arrived near Mars during a
dust storm, because some very valuable
photographs of the progress and decline
of the storm were sent back. For instance, the arc-like features shown in the
picture of Ascraeus Lacus (left) are
certainly due to dusty material, and the
same sort of phenomenon was seen in
other areas, notably the very high Nodus
Gordii. As yet there is no direct knowledge of the sizes of the particles responsible for the obscurations, but they
must be small; otherwise they would not
be whipped up from the surface by the
winds.

The problem of the dust storms is
fundamental to our understanding of
Mars, and probably we will not obtain
full information until it is possible to
carry out observations from the surface
of the planet — a phase of operations
which should begin in 1976 with the
soft-landing of the U.S. Viking probe
(see pages 46 and 47).

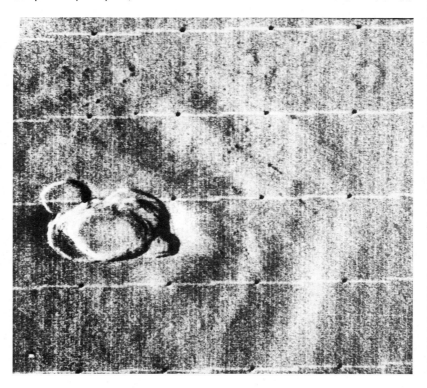

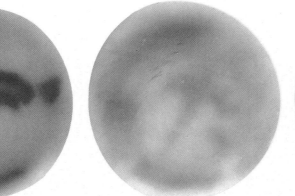

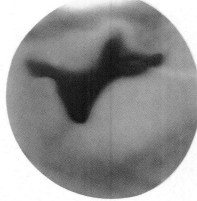

The latest information radically changed opinions about Mars. The old idea of Mars having a relatively featureless landscape, with no major irregularities, has proved to be very wide of the mark. This was obvious as soon as the first clear pictures were received from Mariner 4, in 1965, showing craters. Only a a small part of the surface was photographed by this first probe, but more detailed surveys were carried out by Mariners 6 and 7 in 1969, and with Mariner 9, in 1971–2, excellent charts of most of the surface became available.

The existence of craters led to the suggestion that instead of being basically Earthlike, Mars was similar to the Moon. This may be true, but there are important differences, and some of the structures seen on Mars are unlike anything to be found either on the Moon or on the Earth.

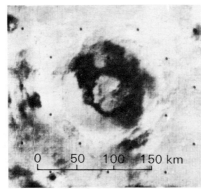

Comparison of Craters *above* The top photograph shows Crater Lake, Oregon, U.S.A. This is a volcanic caldera whose floor is now hidden by water. Both the lunar crater, Tsiolkovskii (left), and the Martian crater in Phaethontis (right), closely resemble Crater Lake, although they are much larger (the Martian crater is 125 km in diameter). It is generally believed that the dark area inside Tsiolkovskii is due to a lake of solidified lava, and the Martian crater is almost certainly volcanic.

The topography of Mars is certainly not homogeneous. There are definite types of terrain, some of which seem to be peculiar to Mars. The craters are dominant in many areas, and, as with the Moon, there can be no doubt that they are of two different kinds: some are volcanic, while others are due to meteoritic impact.

In addition, there are heavily faulted and raised areas, such as that of Ophir-Eos, near the equator of the planet. Near the poles there are indications of what may be thick sedimentary or permafrost areas, covering geological structures of the type seen clearly at lower latitudes.

The largest volcanic structures are different from those of the Moon, and are more massive than anything comparable on Earth. The largest volcano on Earth is Mauna Loa, in the Hawaiian group. This rises to a height of 9·3 km from the sea bed, and has an oval crater at its summit some 4·8 km long. The complex, multiple volcanic crater at the summit of Nix Olympica is 65 km in diameter. The difference demonstrates the colossal scale of some of the Martian volcanic structures. Nix Olympica, seen on the opposite page, is one of the most spectacular of these volcanic mountains and stands in the centre of a region which is relatively smooth and contains many volcanic features. To the south-east there is a great chain of volcanic mountains, stretching 3000 km or more, which gives rise to many interesting theories about the geological nature of Mars, which are discussed more fully in the following pages.

Vulcanism

No active vulcanism has as yet been detected by the instruments on the various spacecraft that have examined Mars, but there must presumably have been activity not so very long ago on the geological time-scale, and it has been suggested – though without proof – that volcanic activity is periodical. In this case, during active periods, with materials being sent out from volcanic vents, the atmosphere may be temporarily denser than it is during the present epoch. An alternative theory is that like the Earth, Mars has experienced a series of 'ice ages', with intervening warmer eras, caused by precession of the polar axis, so that every 25,000 years or so much of the carbon dioxide and most of the ice is evaporated from the poles, to give a temporary increase in the density of the atmosphere. (Precession is the phenomenon by which the direction of the planet's axis describes a circle, over a period of years.) Each period would last for several thousands of years, and would have profound effects upon the surface features.

Height Surveys

Surveys of the height of surface features have been carried out both by radar and by measuring the amount of carbon dioxide existing over different areas. Since the Martian atmosphere is mainly carbon dioxide, this latter method is reliable. An example is given in the illustration below. The two lines of research give very similar results. Elevations of at least 20 km above the mean level (the height of Nix Olympica) have been found. In comparison, Mount Everest is much lower, being only 9 km above sea level. There are also deep depressions: for instance, the famous plain of Hellas has a floor 2 to 3 km lower than the surround-point on the surface – compared with the Earth, an immense range of altitude.

Tithonius Lacus Rift Valley *left* This chasm is situated just south of the Martian equator, between longitudes 90° and 95°, and is one of the deepest clefts on the surface of Mars. The cross-section beneath the photograph was obtained by measuring the amount of carbon dioxide in the atmosphere at different points along a straight line, and computing the height or depth of the surface relative to a mean level. In this photograph (part of the mosaic on page 22) north is to the right. The greatest depth amounts to 5800 metres, and the variations in height in the carbon dioxide cross-section correspond closely to the visible topographical features.

Nix Olympica *right* Photographed in January 1972. This feature, visible from Earth as a tiny speck, has proved to be a gigantic volcano with a base 500 km across, associated with very extensive lava flows spreading over 1000 km. It is much larger than the Hawaiian structure on Earth, and is about 25 km high. Steep cliffs drop off from the mountain flanks to the plain below. At the summit of the structure is a complex, multiple volcanic crater, 65 km in diameter.

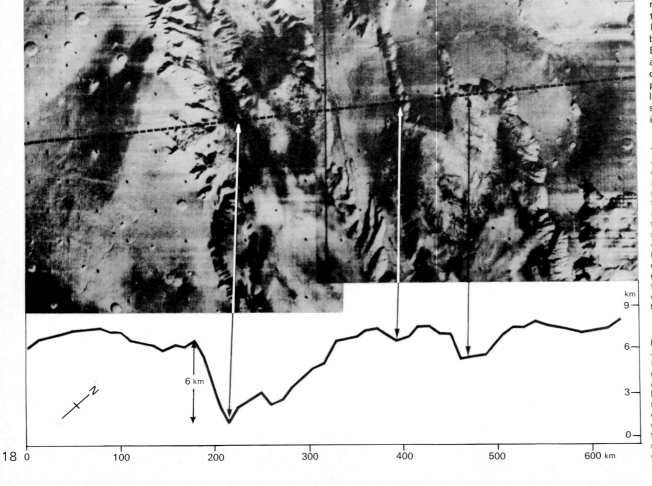

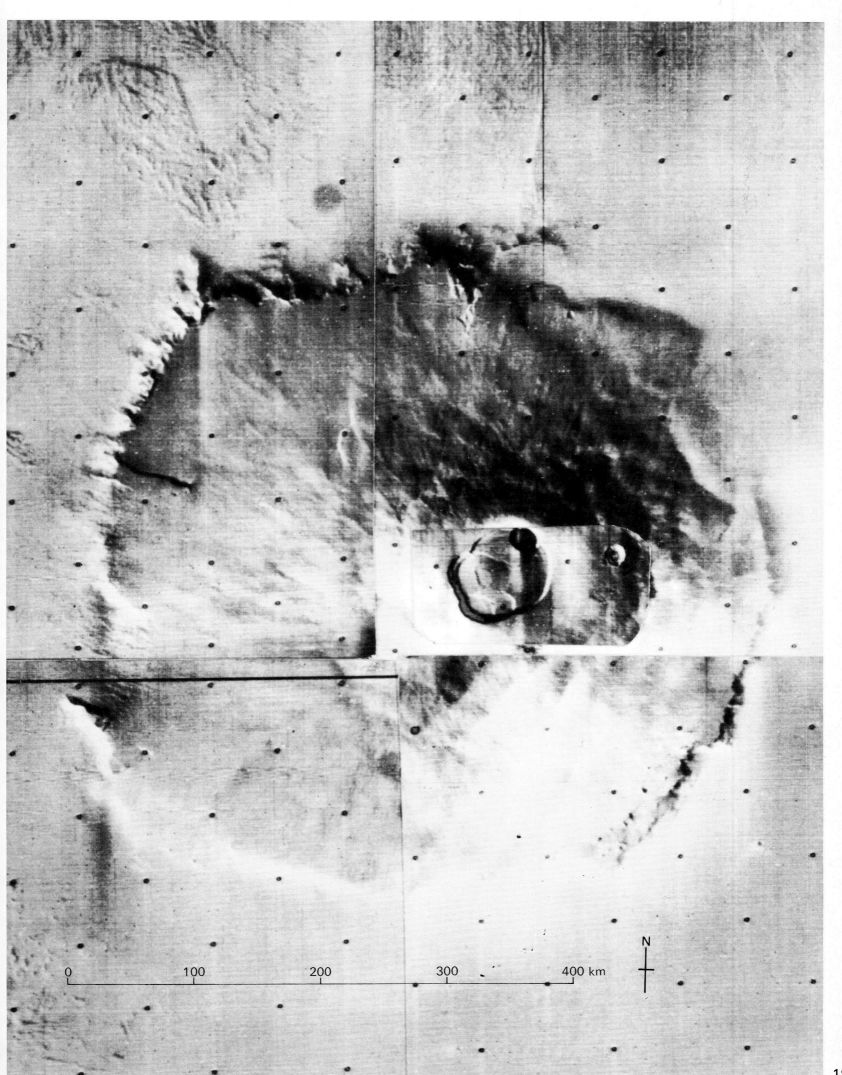

0   100   200   300   400 km

N

Given the major differences described on the previous page, there are also some interesting points of similarity. On Mars, as on our own world, there is an obvious difference between the two hemispheres. On the Earth, most of the great oceans lie south of the equator, with the major land-masses to the north. On Mars, it is found that almost all the massive volcanoes are in the northern hemisphere; only two volcanoes of any size south of the equator are to be seen on the charts in this book. On the other hand, the prominent basins such as Hellas, Argyre I and Thyle I lie to the south, while the major system of rift valleys associated with Tithonius Lacus is not far from the Martian equator. Conditions of this sort have to be borne in mind when trying to formulate ideas about the development and present state of Martian topography.

Two maps, of contrasting regions, are given on the opposite page. One shows Hellas, formerly believed to be a plateau and now known to be the deepest depression so far measured on Mars; it is not likely that any are deeper, since the bottom of the floor goes down 3000 metres below the mean level. (Argyre I is of the same general type, but probably rather less deep, though no accurate figures are available.) The second map shows Tharsis, the area of the huge volcanoes Nodus Gordii, Pavonis Lacus and Ascraeus Lacus; of these the first is one of the highest points so far on Mars (over 20 km above the mean).

Nix Olympica *below* The atmospheric dust has started to subside, but is still evident. The upper photograph shows an area of 440 km × 560 km. Below is a telephoto picture covering an area 43 km × 55 km, located inside the inscribed rectangle above. The feathery texture and small intersecting elongated lobes indicate a flow of material down the slope away from the central crater complex.

More recent work suggests that initial surveys may have underestimated the true vertical scale of the Martian topography by up to 50 per cent.

From a purely topographical point of view, the famous dark areas visible from Earth, such as the Syrtis Major, are lost when we examine a chart based on the close-range Mariner information. Only a few features, such as Hellas and Argyre I, are recognisable at a glance. In revising opinions about Mars it is worth making a closer comparison with the Earth in view of recent discussions about plate tectonics.

Plate Tectonics
Plate tectonics makes up a comparatively new branch of geology. Basically, it is assumed that the surface of the Earth is made up of a discrete number of large, thick, rocky plates, which move about slowly on top of the viscous material below. Originally, all the land masses were combined into one supercontinent (known to geologists as Pan-

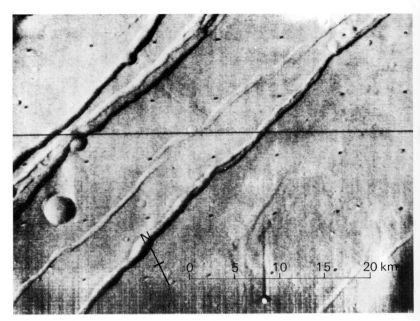

Rills in the Mare Sirenum *above* The widest rill, at the upper left, is 1·6 km in width; the whole system of parallel fissures extends for over 1800 km. The picture was taken from a distance of 1730 km, and covers an area of 34 × 43 km.

gaea), and in the remote past this super-continent split up. Since then, plate movements have been responsible for features such as mountain ranges, produced when one plate collides with another. The study is really a development of the continental drift theory, proposed in 1917 by Wegener, who realised that (for instance) Africa and South America should fit together according to their coastlines. There is much evidence in favour of plate tectonics. There is also much that is tentative, that remains to be proved. It is, therefore, important to see whether the principle can also be applied to Mars. It is first necessary to see whether the two globes are alike inside, with liquid cores — otherwise the shifting rock-plate theory cannot apply.

Plate Tectonics applied to Mars
Recent probe findings indicate that Mars has a magnetic field, if only a weak one. This may well mean that the planet really does have a liquid core analogous to the heavy nickel-iron core of the Earth, though it is presumably smaller. On this score, then, there is no obvious reason why plate tectonics should not apply there.

There is evidence of a Martian grid system. For instance, the lines of volcanoes in Tharsis and Tempe trend from the south-west to the north-east, as does the ridge system of Tractus Albus. We may therefore look in particular at the great northern volcanoes. Nodus Gordii is more massive and loftier than Ascraeus Lacus, still further to the north-east; and the chain of volcanoes is continued, with decreasing size, down to the scattered cones in the area of Tempe. Presumably Nodus Gordii is the oldest of these, and the small Tempe formations the youngest.

According to one theory of plate tec-tonics, a volcano may be produced by an underground source of heat, which penetrates the plate above and finally produces a volcano. Some of the Pacific chain of volcanoes are examples of this. Let us assume that this applied on Mars, and that Nodus Gordii was formed in such a way. Assume also that the plate upon which it arose was moving south-west. As the plate moved, the heat source would finally be below another weak point north-east of the first and Pavonic Lacus would be produced, though since it would be younger the heat source would have used up some of its original energy — and the volcano would be less massive. With further shifting of the plate, Ascraeus Lacus would come into being, and so on. Finally, with the decrease of the heat source, the volcanoes formed would be very small, and production would eventually cease altogether. This explanation would seem plausible when applied to Nodus Gordii chain, and would also account for the Tractus Albus ridge system.

Other Volcanic Areas
With the colossal Nix Olympica, the process would be different, since a different plate would be involved. Nix Olympica is particularly extensive, and its influence has spread over a wide area, with more ancient features being covered up by lava flows and volcanic debris. There are also differences in Elysium, the other major volcanic area in the northern hemisphere, and the areas south of Propontis and Ismenius Lacus are much older, so that the original effects have been largely masked by later cratering.

Since Mariner 9 completed its programme in October 1972, and it will be some years before another comparable spacecraft reaches Mars (at least from America) we must simply wait to see whether these ideas are valid. The best we can say at the moment is that if plate tectonics can explain many of the Earth's features, it must also be tested with regard to Mars.

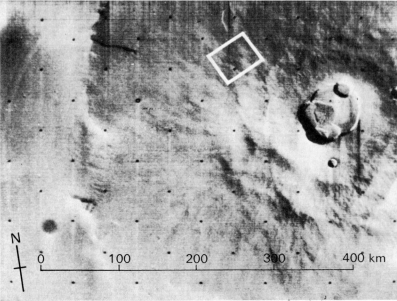

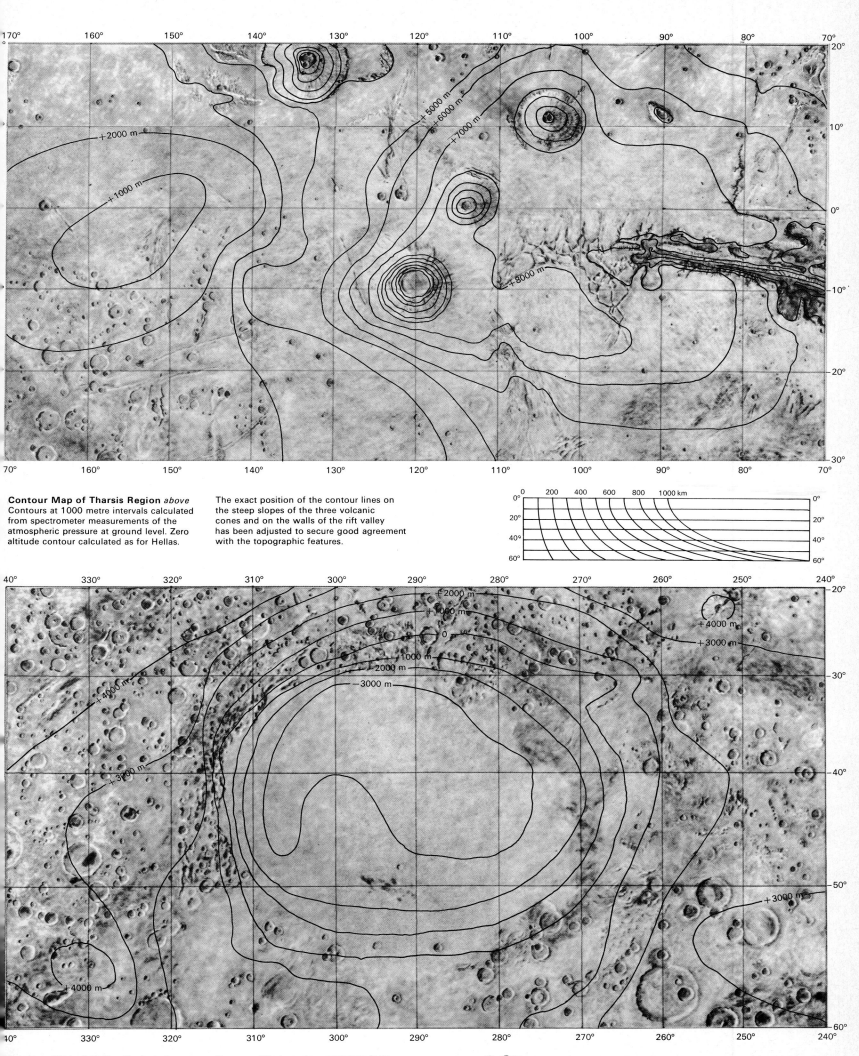

Contour Map of Tharsis Region *above*
Contours at 1000 metre intervals calculated
from spectrometer measurements of the
atmospheric pressure at ground level. Zero
altitude contour calculated as for Hellas.

The exact position of the contour lines on
the steep slopes of the three volcanic
cones and on the walls of the rift valley
has been adjusted to secure good agreement
with the topographic features.

Contour Map of Hellas Region *above*
Contours at 1000 metre intervals
calculated from spectrometer measurements
of the atmospheric pressure at ground level.

The zero altitude contour corresponds to
the triple point of water (6·15 millibars).
Above this level, water can only exist as
solid or vapour; below it, as a liquid.

21

TOPOGRAPHY 3

The valleys shown here all lie in the south-western quadrant of Mars, and are very extensive. The main rift valley, extending from Tithonius Lacus through Melas Lacus and Coprates, is situated to the east of the massive volcanoes of which Nodus Gordii and Nix Olympica are the loftiest. To the west of the volcanoes are some much less prominent valleys, extending near Gorgonum Sinus from Memnonia into Mare Sirenum. Here, too, the slope of the ground is downhill from the volcanoes; it is at least possible that the rills are of the same nature as the great rift valley, but much less developed.

Much can be learned from a careful examination of the details in these Mariner 9 photographs. The rills to the west of the volcanic highlands are too delicate to be seen from Earth; they are nowhere more than 2 km wide, which is well below the resolving power of even our largest telescopes. However, the rift valley area to the east of the volcanoes is very different. The maximum breadth is 400 km, with a mean depth of 5 to 7 km.

This area, and the three circular features toward the edge of the valley at the left of the mosaic, have been recorded telescopically as dark patches, and so we have a reliable correlation between colour and depth — at least in this instance.

From a geological point of view, it is obviously of crucial importance to decide how these valleys and rills were formed. There is a close superficial analogy between the western rills and the rills on the Moon, but there is nothing on the Moon comparable with the eastern rift valley system, and on examining the photographs it is difficult to avoid the conclusion that the system itself was formed as a typical rift valley by movement of the crust, and was subsequently extensively modified by the action of liquid — presumably water. This theory is made more plausible by the fact that the massive volcanoes stand at the highest end of the system, and that the valleys run 'downhill' all the way until the system ends in the region of Chryse.

Yet there is less erosion than would be expected if the system were geologically very old. Therefore, if water were involved, it follows that conditions on Mars must have been very different in relatively recent times (that is to say, a few hundreds of thousands of years ago).

So far as is known, the Tithonius Lacus rift valley system is the most extensive on Mars, though there are plenty of smaller examples of the same type of structure.

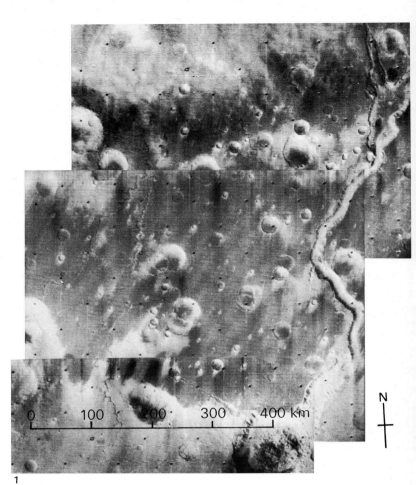

1

3

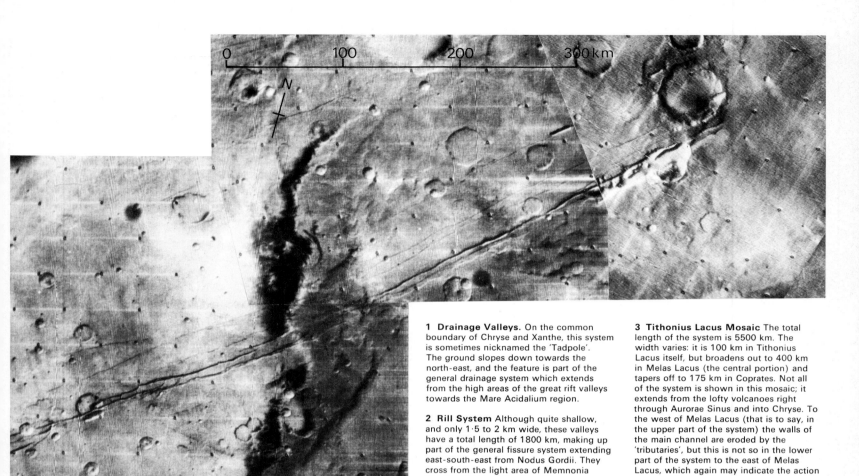

1 Drainage Valleys. On the common boundary of Chryse and Xanthe, this system is sometimes nicknamed the 'Tadpole'. The ground slopes down towards the north-east, and the feature is part of the general drainage system which extends from the high areas of the great rift valleys towards the Mare Acidalium region.

2 Rill System Although quite shallow, and only 1·5 to 2 km wide, these valleys have a total length of 1800 km, making up part of the general fissure system extending east-south-east from Nodus Gordii. They cross from the light area of Memnonia into the region of the Mare Sirenum.

3 Tithonius Lacus Mosaic The total length of the system is 5500 km. The width varies: it is 100 km in Tithonius Lacus itself, but broadens out to 400 km in Melas Lacus (the central portion) and tapers off to 175 km in Coprates. Not all of the system is shown in this mosaic; it extends from the lofty volcanoes right through Aurorae Sinus and into Chryse. To the west of Melas Lacus (that is to say, in the upper part of the system) the walls of the main channel are eroded by the 'tributaries', but this is not so in the lower part of the system to the east of Melas Lacus, which again may indicate the action of water flowing down the slope.

2

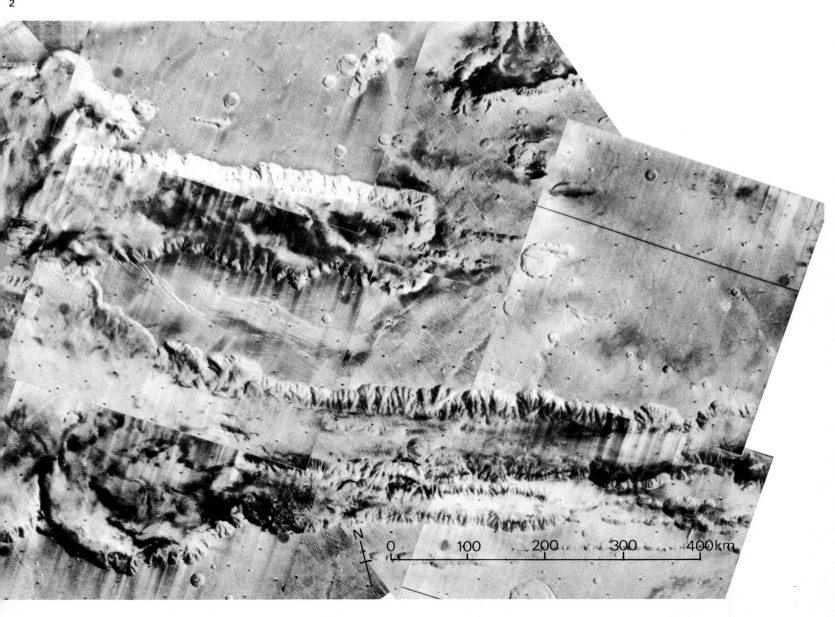

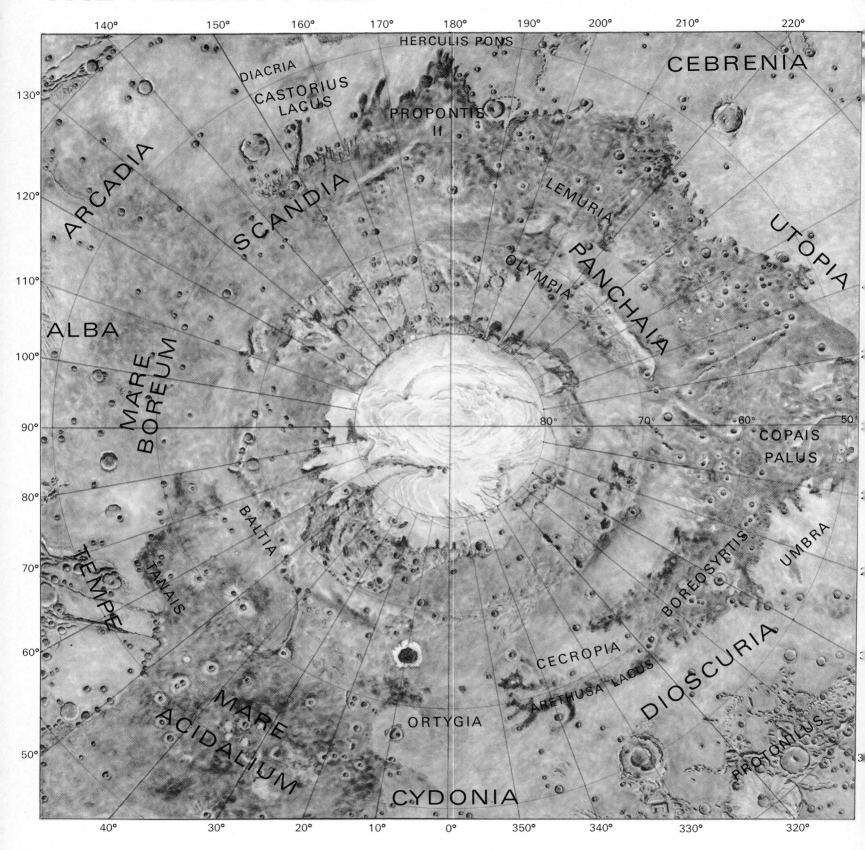

The north polar cap is smaller than the southern cap, but it never vanishes entirely. Even in the middle of Martian summer some white deposit remains. Mariner 9 photographs have greatly extended knowledge of the area: some were taken when the northern cap had shrunk and was clearly visible in the absence of atmospheric obscuration. The boundary of the summer cap is seen to be a roughish, dark area; further towards the pole itself are the strange spiral features which are associated with structures on the surface, even though they are never free from whiteness.

The polar caps were formerly thought to be made up of water ice, though it was known that their thickness was slight. Were they deep, they could never melt (or sublime) under the influence of of the weak solar radiation, and they release very little water vapour into the atmosphere. Nowadays it seems more or less certain that the main constituent is solid carbon dioxide, although since whiteness can persist at times when the temperature is high enough to make carbon dioxide sublime, we may assume that at least a small amount of ordinary ice is present.

The Northern Hemisphere *right* This Mariner 9 mosaic is made up of three photographs, taken from an average range of 13,700 km in August 1972. It shows the area from the pole to a few degrees south of the equator. The area is free from atmospheric obscuration, as the dust storm of the previous autumn had cleared.

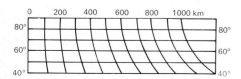

Distances may be measured by using that scale in the scale diagram which corresponds to the latitude of the mid-point of the measured distance.
Scale: 1:23,500,000 at the equator

The coloured area on the globe indicates the area referred to in the chart.

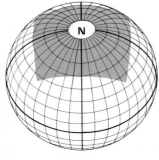

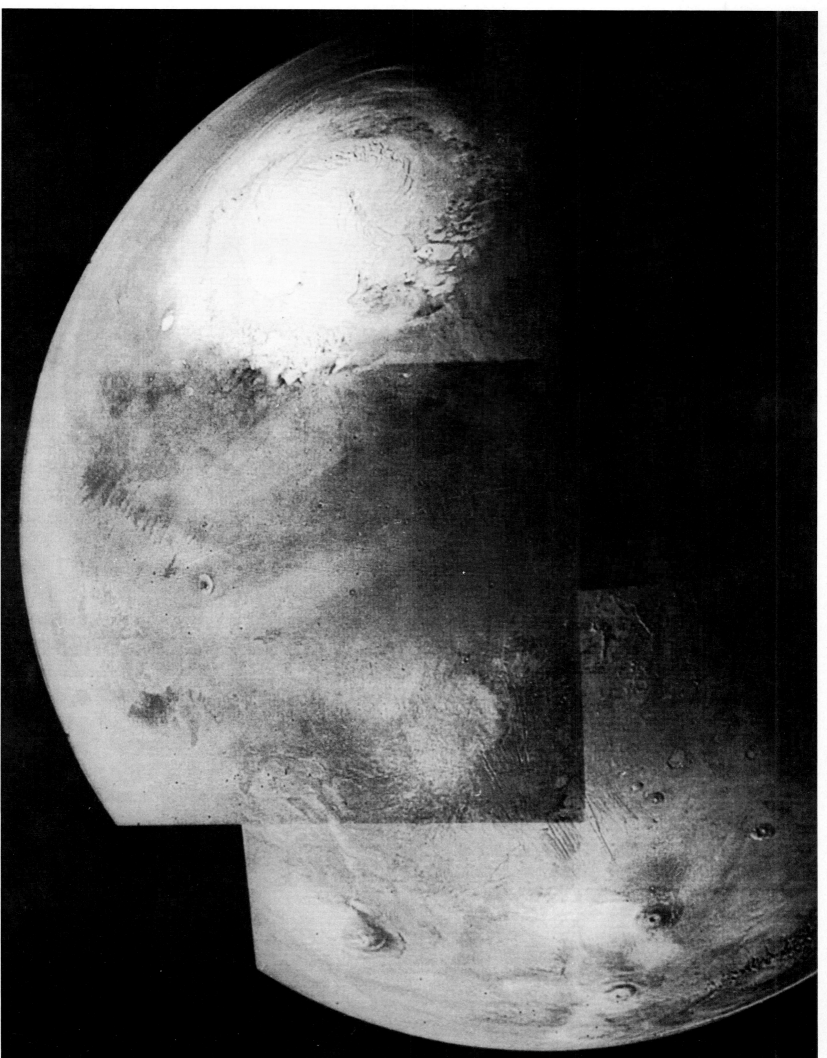

THE NORTH-WEST QUADRANT

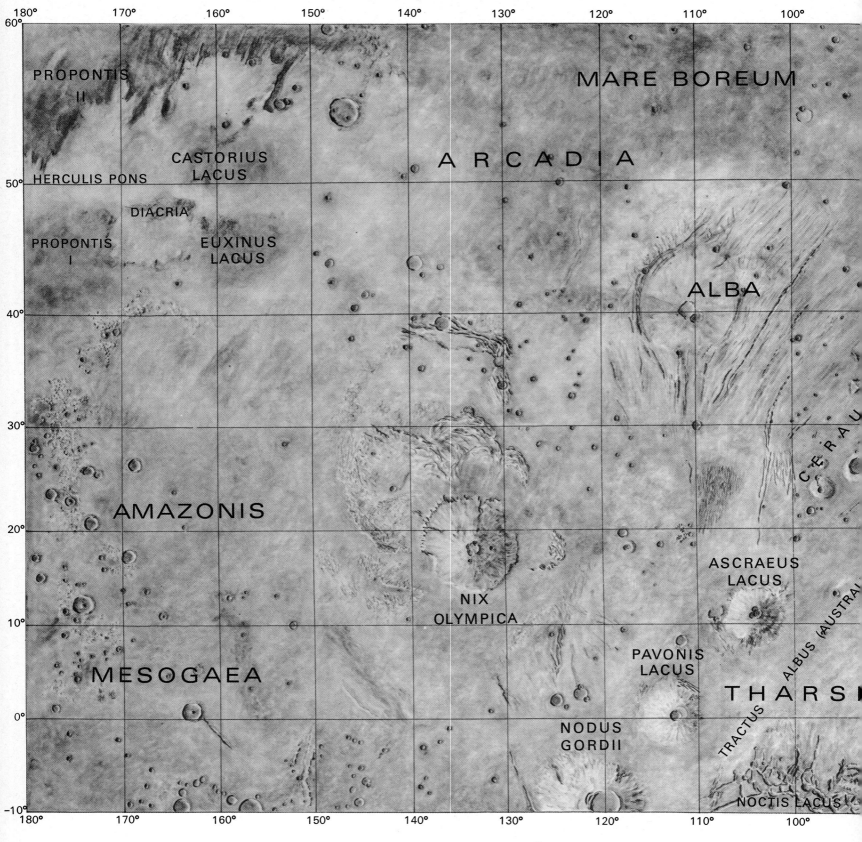

180°   170°   160°   150°   140°   130°   120°   110°   100°

MARE BOREUM

PROPONTIS
II

A R C A D I A

CASTORIUS
LACUS

HERCULIS PONS

DIACRIA

PROPONTIS
I

EUXINUS
LACUS

ALBA

AMAZONIS

C E R A U

ASCRAEUS
LACUS

NIX
OLYMPICA

PAVONIS
LACUS

ALBUS (AUSTRA

MESOGAEA

T H A R S I

NODUS
GORDII

TRACTUS

NOCTIS LACUS

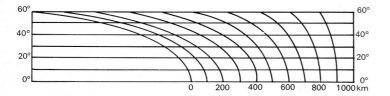

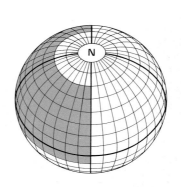

Distances may be measured by using that
scale in the scale diagram which
corresponds to the latitude of the mid-point
of the measured distance.
Scale: 1:23,500,000 at the equator

The coloured area on the globe indicates
the area referred to in the chart.

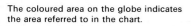

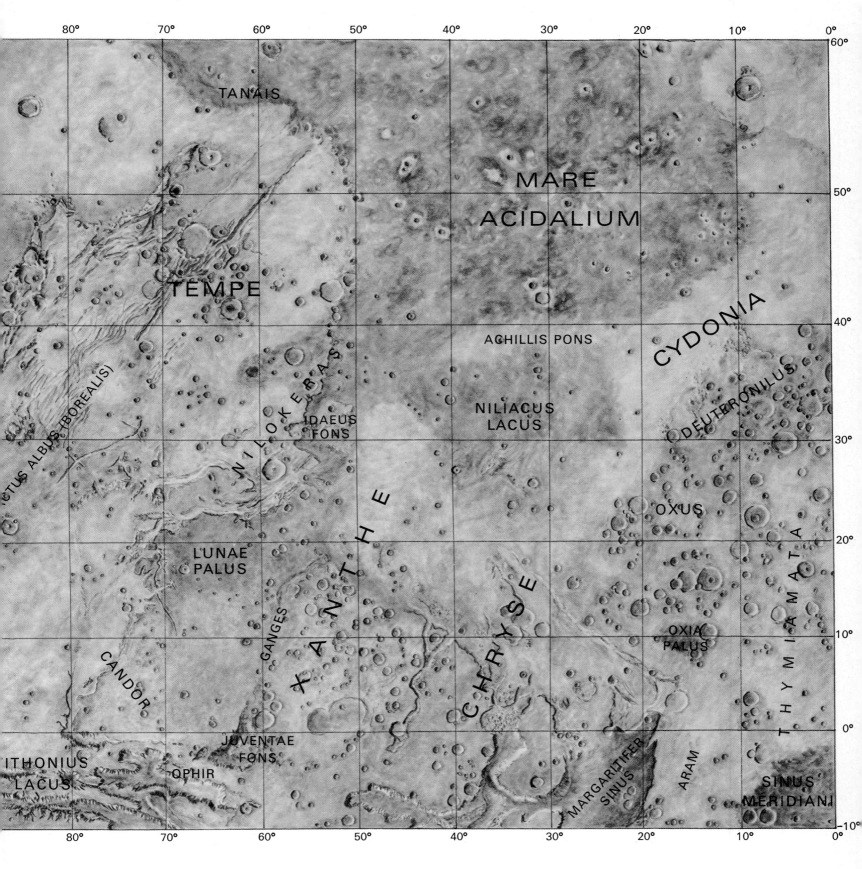

TANAIS

MARE
ACIDALIUM

TEMPE

CYDONIA

ACHILLIS PONS

DEUTERONILUS

NILIACUS
LACUS

NILOKERAS

IDAEUS
FONS

(LACTUS ALBUS (BOREALIS)

OXUS

L'UNAE
PALUS

X A N T H E

C H R Y S E

OXIA
PALUS

GANGES

CANDOR

T H Y M I A M A T A

JUVENTAE
FONS

ITHONIUS
LACUS

OPHIR

MARGARITIFER
SINUS

ARAM

SINUS
MERIDIANI

This area contains many features of special significance. There is Tithonius Lacus, described in detail on page 23, together with the lofty Nodus Gordii and the massive volcano of Nix Olympica. Also in the area is the Mare Acidalium, which, as seen from Earth, is the most prominent dark feature on Mars apart from the Syrtis Major.

The general slope of the ground shows the existence of extensive drainage systems. Basically, the Tithonius Lacus and Nix Olympica areas are high, and slope off in all directions, although the slope downward to the west (toward Amazonis and Mesogaea) is much steeper than to the east (Chryse, Thymiamata) or north (Mare Acidalium). The Lunae Palus is high, while the Mare

Acidalium is depressed; yet from Earth the two appear of much the same colour – a reminder that surface tint is no key to elevation. The old idea of all dark areas being depressed sea beds is clearly untenable. Further drainage systems extend from the Chryse region down to Niliacus Lacus, a dark patch which joins on to the Mare Acidalium.

One feature of note is the Tractus Albus, which extends across Tharsis and Tempe. It has been seen from Earth; it was first recorded as long ago as 1879 by Schiaparelli, who described it as a streak 4000 km in length, forming a Y with Candor, and it was also described by later observers (including one of the present authors, using a 30 cm reflector). It stretches from near Nodus Gordii as

far as the Mare Acidalium, and is essentially a ridge. It is undoubtedly associated with the diagonal line of volcanoes to the west of it (Nodus Gordii, Pavonis Lacus, Ascraeus Lacus and others across Tempe) which are of decreasing size, and presumably decreasing age, from south to north.

The whole western area of this map is dominated by the high volcanic region centred upon Nix Olympica. It is evident that all around this is an area, roughly circular, which is comparatively free of major craters. It includes Amazonis and Mesogaea to the west, but is also identifiable in other directions. The relatively small craters in these regions are almost certainly best explained as impact pits, not directly associated

with the tectonic systems.

Also of significance in the volcanic areas are the lava flows, which are widespread and well marked. They are particularly well developed round the Nix Olympica, which proves to be a much more extensive structure than might be thought by looking only at photographs of the main volcano. Undoubtedly the structure has had a great modifying influence over a wide region.

In the north, the Mare Acidalium extends beyond this chart towards the pole; so does the dark, less well defined region of the Mare Boreum, which appears to be low lying. The northern parts of these dark areas are, of course, covered with polar deposit during winter in the northern hemisphere of Mars.

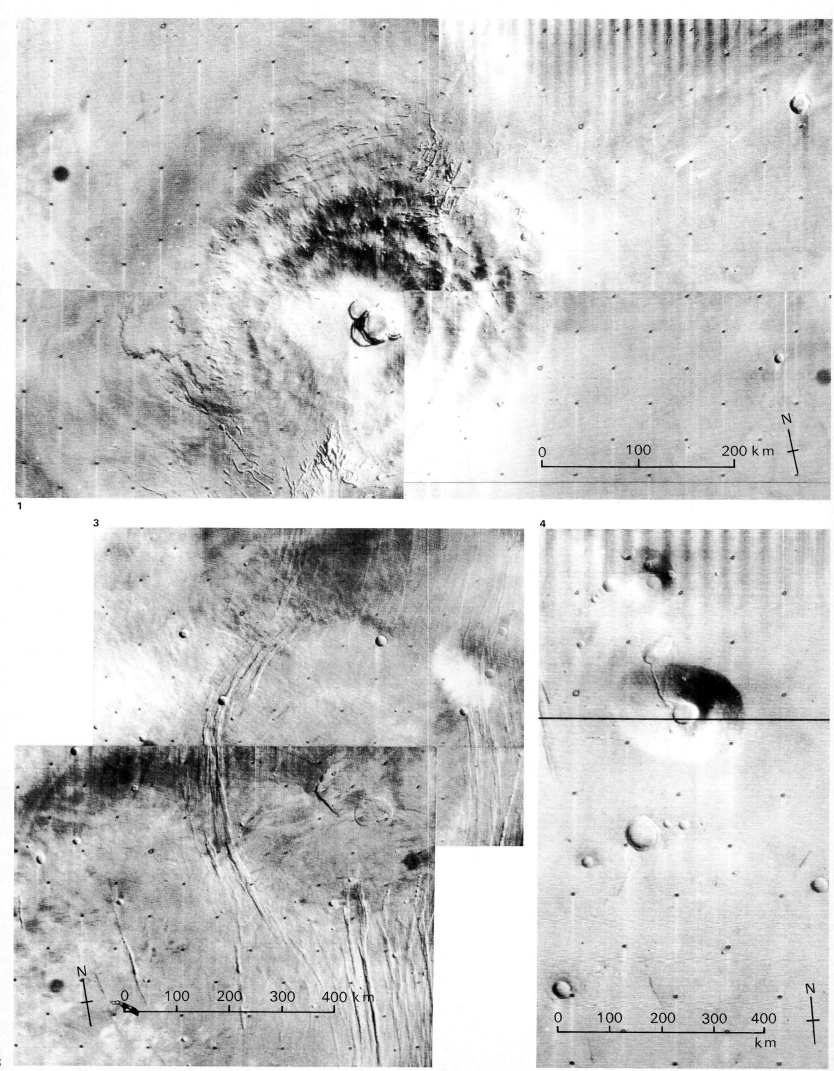

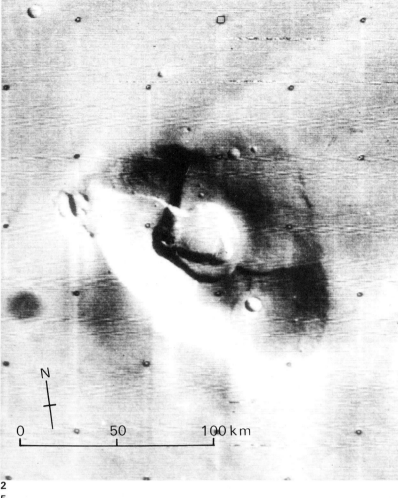

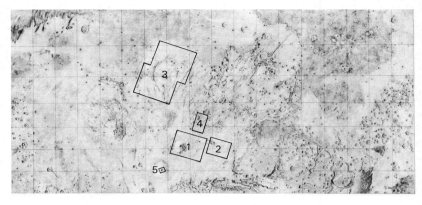

1 Ascraeus Lacus This is one of the
great line of volcanic structures in the area
dominated by Nix Olympica. Ascraeus
Lacus lies to the north of Pavonis Lacus,
and, like it, consists of a volcano topped
by a complex caldera. It is of considerable
altitude, and so was one of the first
features to be photographed from Mariner 9
when the dust storm began to subside.

2 Volcano east of Ascraeus Lacus
This is a relatively small volcanic cone,
with a base 160 km across and a 70 km
caldera. It lies 780 km east of Ascraeus
Lacus, close to Tractus Albus. The shape of
the structure has been distorted; it is
elongated to the south-east, and there is a
secondary cone, with its own well marked
caldera, on the flank of the main volcano.

3 Alba Almost due north of Ascraeus
Lacus, Alba is a volcanic structure of
somewhat different type. There is a low,
rather gently sloping dome, and a
shallower crater structure at the summit.
The altitude is also much less than that of
the giant volcanoes to the south, and the
ground in this area slopes toward the

relatively low areas of the polar regions.
Some of the striations in the terrain seem
to go round Alba itself – elsewhere they
tend to be grouped in parallels.

4 Volcanoes in Ceraunius Volcanic
structures, making up part of the long line
which begins in the south at Nodus
Gordii and extends in a north-east direction
through the border areas of Tharsis and
Tempe as far as Mare Acidalium. Also
visible on this photograph (and on the
main map) are more of the curious parallel
ridges and valleys.

5 Pavonis Lacus Pavonis Lacus is the
central member of the three main
volcanoes of the great diagonal system;
it lies between Nodus Gordii and Ascraeus
Lacus, and when the first Mariner 9
pictures were released it was nicknamed
'Middle Spot'. The summit crater is 40 km
in diameter, and the whole structure is
undoubtedly a shield volcano; the smooth
crater floor is probably a lake of solidified
lava. The photograph here was taken on
10 January 1972, at a distance of 1950 km,
with the telephoto lens.

2
5

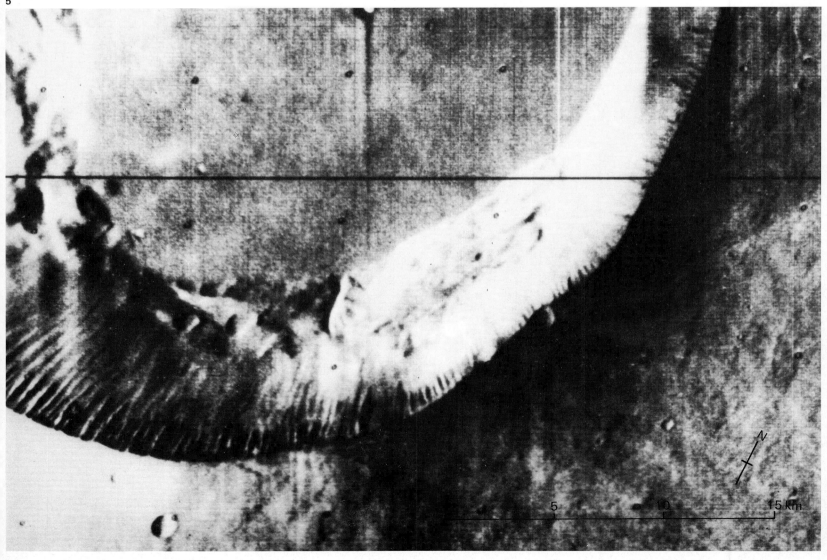

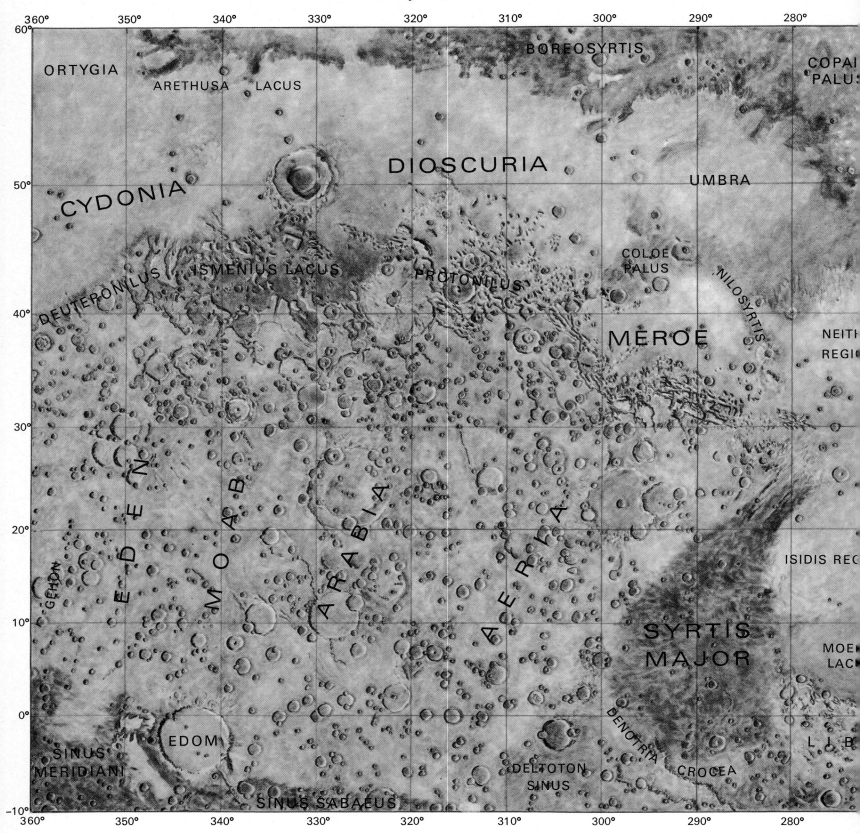

BOREOSYRTIS

COPAIS
PALUS

ARETHUSA LACUS

DIOSCURIA

CYDONIA

UMBRA

COLOE
PALUS

NILOSYRTIS

DEUTERONILUS

ISMENIUS LACUS

PROTONILUS

MEROE

NEITH
REGIO

E D E N

M O A B

A R A B I A

A E R I A

MEROE

GEHON

SYRTIS
MAJOR

ISIDIS REG

MOE
LAC

EDOM

DELTOTON
SINUS

OENOTRIA

CROCEA

LIB

SINUS
MERIDIANI

SINUS SABAEUS

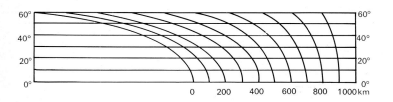

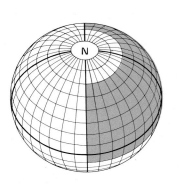

Distances may be measured by using that
scale in the scale diagram which
corresponds to the latitude of the mid-point
of the measured distance.
Scale: 1:23,500,000 at the equator

The coloured area on the globe indicates
the area referred to in the chart.

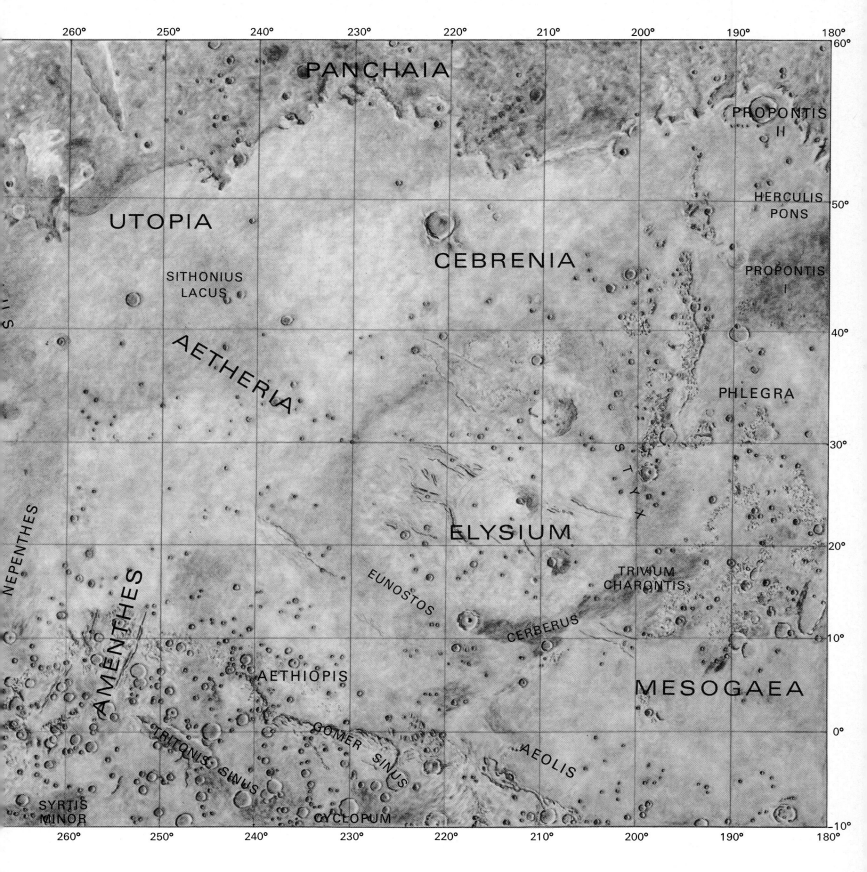

This whole quadrant is dominated by the Syrtis Major, which is much the most prominent dark feature on Mars as seen from the Earth, and was the first to be recorded telescopically (by Huygens, in the 17th century). It had always been regarded as a deep depression, possibly a sea bed, but in fact it is nothing of the kind. It is a relatively smooth area, and takes the form of a plateau, sloping off to either side. What is more remarkable is that on the Mariner photographs, there is nothing to distinguish the Syrtis Major apart from its colour. The same applies to the Sinus Meridiani, which appears to the extreme north-west of the chart.

North of the Syrtis Major is Casius, nicknamed 'the Wedge', also prominent from the Earth; the ground here is much lower, as the slope is northward toward the polar zone, and Casius, like Syrtis Major, is simply an albedo feature. This applies also to the dark streak of the Nilosyrtis, which is undoubtedly one of Lowell's so-called 'canals'.

To the west of the Syrtis Major is an ancient and heavily cratered highland area, including Aeria, Arabia, Moab and Eden. The area called Edom has been seen as a small patch; Mariner photographs show it to be a large crater. South of the dark area Ismenius Lacus, not far from Protonilus, there are two or three volcanic cones which have been severely modified by subsequent cratering. Note also the isolated, flat-topped mesas (high tablelands) in the

Ismenius Lacus region. One of these is of distinctive shape; it is 70 km long and 50 km wide (the authors have nicknamed it 'Buckingham Palace').

To the east of Syrtis Major lies the smooth, light-coloured Isidis Regio, bounded by the streak of the Nepenthes — another of Lowell's 'canals', and easily visible from Earth as a broad band, although it also seems to have nothing to mark it in the way of topographical features. Here the general slope of the ground is downward to the north. The photographs show few craters in Aetheria and Cebrenia, although it is possible that there may be more features than are shown here; much depends upon the degree of low-level dust obscuration during the active period of Mariner 9.

Elysium is a volcanic province of intermediate geological age; it contains two volcanic craters and a well marked dome. Adjoining it is the Trivium Charontis, which, as seen from Earth, is of variable intensity. Extending from it are the dark streaks of the Styx and the Cerberus (yet more of Lowell's 'canals', now seen to mark the border of the circular volcanic province of Elysium).

The region north of latitude +55° is mainly dark (Panchaia, Copais Palus, Boreosyrtis) and this darkness extends onto the north-west quadrant (Mare Boreum). It is possible that the dark band may be in part responsible for the dark peripheral region of the polar cap, which was formerly attributed to the effects of melting ice.

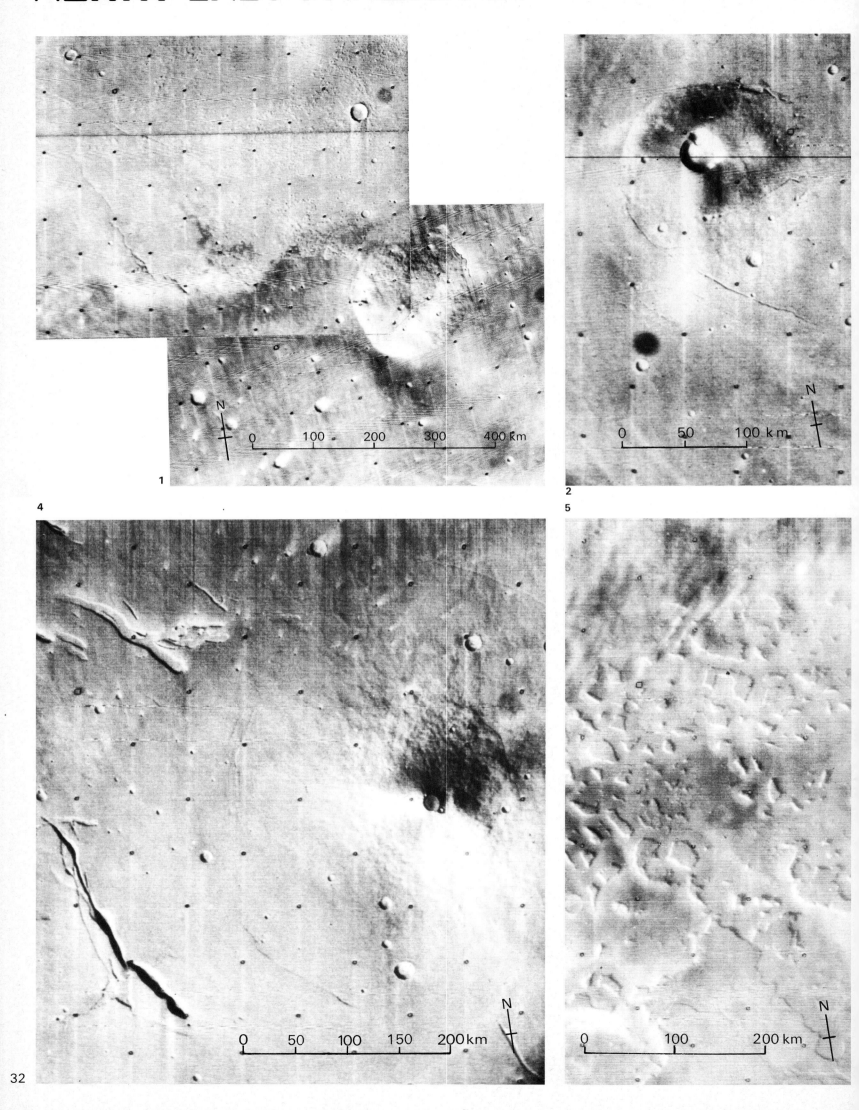

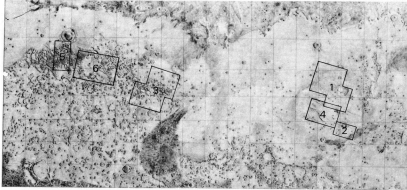

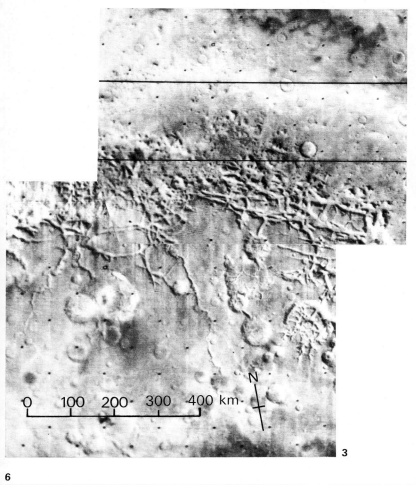

0 100 200 300 400 km

N

3

1 Elysium This is a major volcanic province, though less well marked and presumably older than some of those shown in the north-west quadrant of the planet. This photograph shows a volcanic mountain of the familiar type, topped by a crater, and a much lower volcanic dome. The scattered craters all over the area are probably impact pits.

2 Secondary Volcano in Elysium This volcano lies 350 km south-east of the central features of the plain. It has a base 170 km in diameter and a 58 km summit caldera. To the lower right may be seen the dark area Trivium Charontis, which is familiar to all telescopic observers of Mars.

3 Features in Meroe The valleys and ridges make up what is clearly an orderly pattern, and are included in what may be regarded as a Martian 'grid system'. The region in this photograph lies at the edge of the volcanic area west of Syrtis Major.

4 Central Volcano in Elysium This Mariner 9 photograph shows the main volcano in Elysium, one of the well known light coloured regions of Mars and now found to be essentially volcanic, with complicated drainage features.

5 Features near Ismenius Lacus The region shown here is the edge of an ancient volcanic area, and includes the feature which has been nicknamed 'Buckingham Palace'. To the north of this region is a large crater, on the light area between Dioscuria and Cydonia.

6 Features in Protonilus. This region, to the east of Ismenius Lacus, contains a variety of ancient volcanic structures. The 330 km diameter shield with a composite central caldera (lower middle of the picture) is a typical example. Wave clouds obscuring detail in the north-west corner are the edge of the north polar haze cap.

6

N

0   100   200   300   400 km

THE SOUTH-WEST QUADRANT

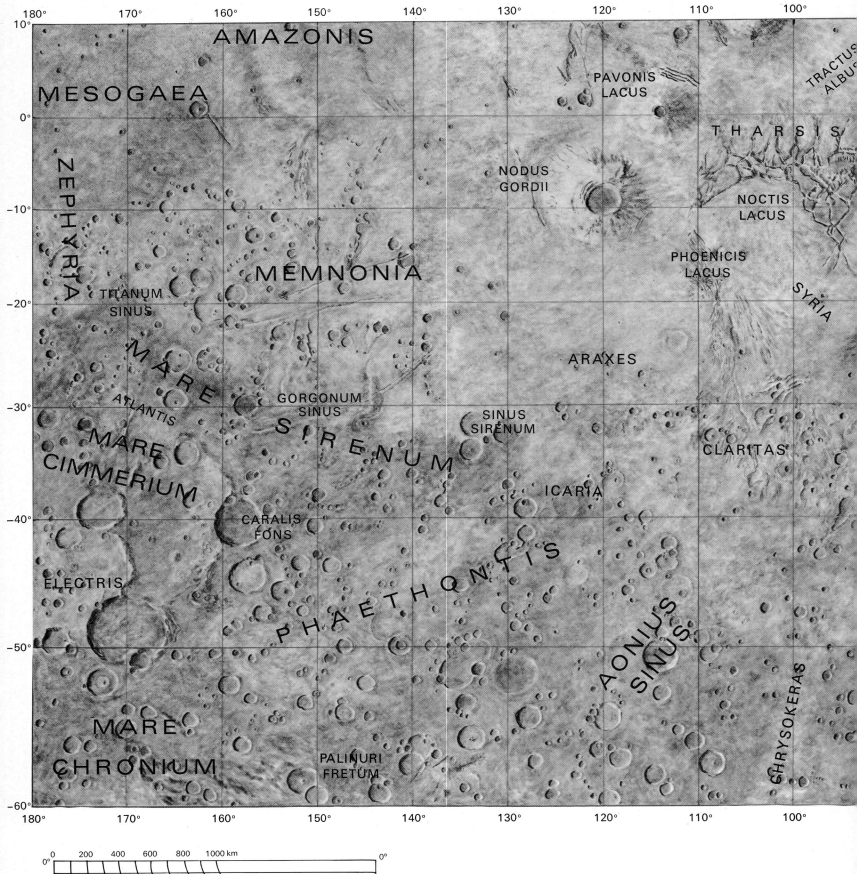

AMAZONIS

MESOGAEA

ZEPHYRIA

TRACTUS ALBUS

PAVONIS LACUS

THARSIS

NODUS GORDII

NOCTIS LACUS

PHOENICIS LACUS

MEMNONIA

SYRIA

TITANUM SINUS

ARAXES

MARE

ATLANTIS

GORGONUM SINUS

SINUS SIRENUM

CLARITAS

SIRENUM

MARE CIMMERIUM

ICARIA

CARALIS FONS

PHAETHONTIS

ELECTRIS

AONIUS SINUS

CHRYSOKERAS

MARE CHRONIUM

PALINURI FRETUM

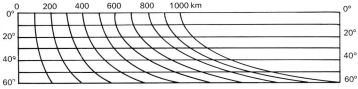

Distances may be measured by using that
scale in the scale diagram which
corresponds to the latitude of the mid-point
of the measured distance.
Scale: 1:23,500,000 at the equator

The coloured area on the globe indicates
the area referred to in the chart.

S

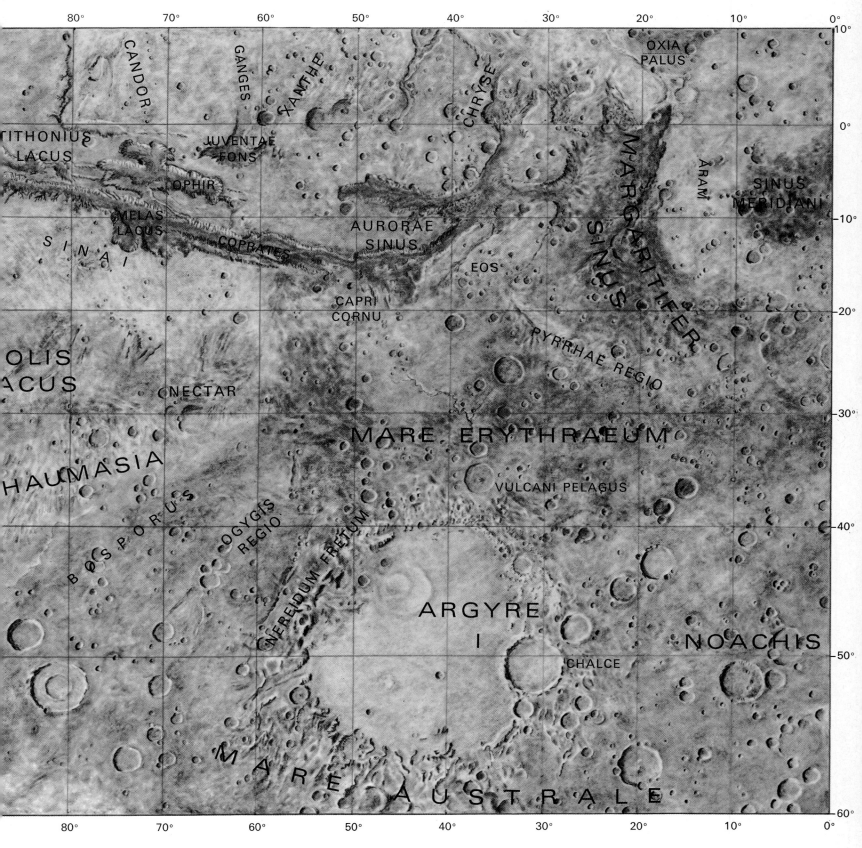

This quadrant includes some of the features most familiar to Earth-based telescopic observers of Mars. The dark Mare Sirenum and Mare Erythraeum are prominent even in small telescopes when the planet is well placed; Mariner photographs show that both are cratered, and in addition Mare Sirenum contains some long, relatively straight valleys or rills.

Another very well known feature is Argyre I, which is a light area and was formerly regarded as a plateau. Height traverses have shown that this is not the case. Like the even more prominent Hellas, Argyre I is a basin, with a relatively featureless interior and a comparatively well marked border — particularly to the north-west, toward

Nereidum Fretum. Argyre I is less deep than Hellas, but it is essentially the same type of formation.

Near the centre of the map is the Solis Lacus, one of the most variable areas on Mars. Telescopic observers from 1877 onward have noted pronounced changes of shape and intensity of the dark patch and photographs of it from future probes will be of great interest.

The quadrant is dominated by the tremendous system of rift valleys extending from near Tharsis through Tithonius Lacus, Melas Lacus, and Coprates over to Aurorae Sinus. If we can decide how they were formed we will be well on the way to a better understanding of the history of the Martian surface. Near the western, high-altitude end of the system

are the lofty volcanic cones of Nodus Gordii and Pavonis Lacus, which are unusual in having unmodified, circular summit craters. Nodus Gordii is the higher of the two. Radar and carbon dioxide traverses agree in giving its height at over 20 km, so that it is certainly one of the loftiest points so far measured anywhere on Mars. Antoniadi noted that it was one of the few features which could still be identified when the planet was still covered with dust; and during the storm of 1971 Nodus Gordii was one of the few objects to remain constantly visible. We now know that there is a simple explanation: the peak is so high that it protrudes above much of the dust.

Other dark features particularly well

known to Earth-based observers are Aurorae Sinus and Margaritifer Sinus, which lie to the east of the main rift valleys. Margaritifer Sinus is easily identifiable on the Mariner photographs because of its colour and its characteristic shape. It is separated from the Sinus Meridiani by the comparatively light area known as Aram.

It was in this quadrant that the Russians brought down the lander of their Mars 3 probe. The impact point was at latitude −45°, longitude −158°, between Eridania and Phaethontis. Unfortunately the lander transmitted for only 20 seconds, and nothing positive was learned from it; but from all accounts the actual landing was successful.

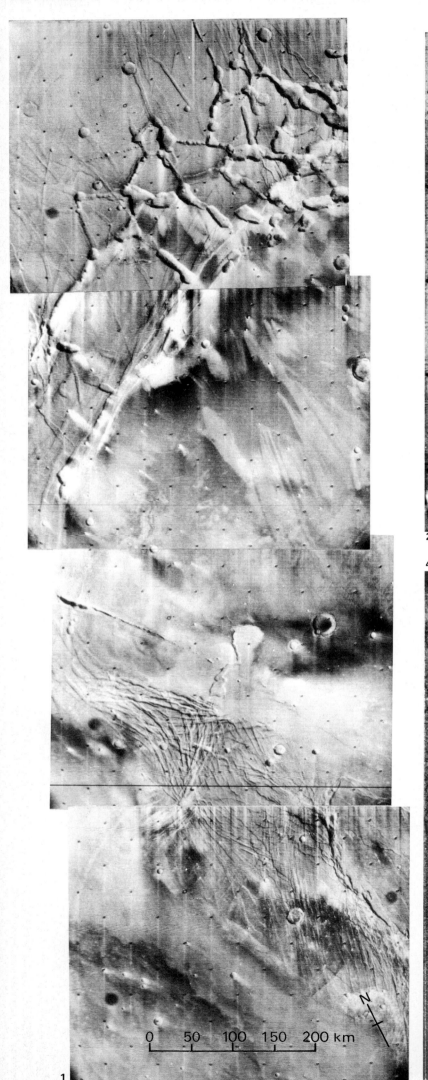

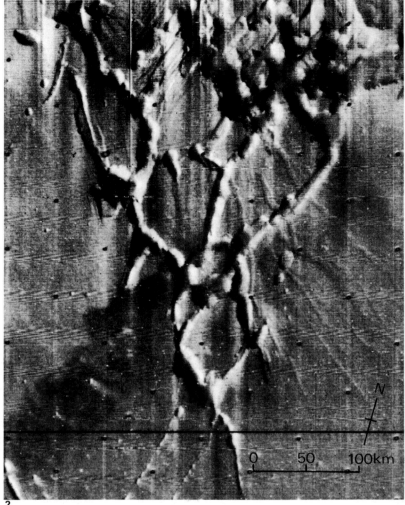

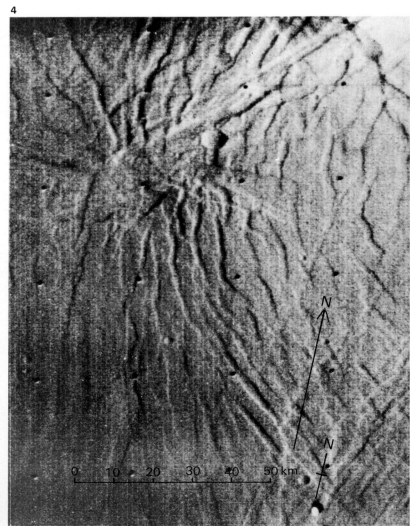

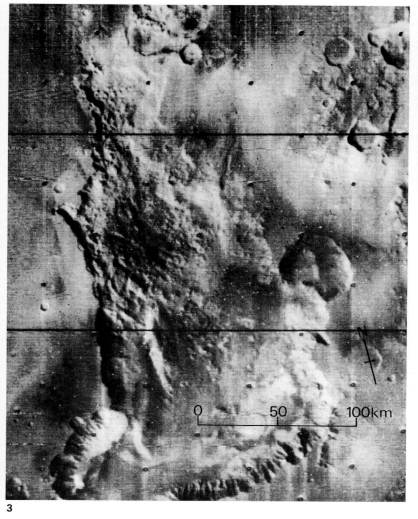

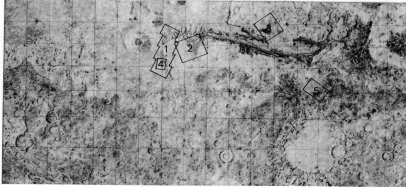

1 Phoenicis Lacus This is an elevated plateau, with a mean height of 5½ km. To the south are systems of intersecting fault valleys; each valley is about 2½ km wide. There are few craters; the surface may be covered with relatively young volcanic deposits. To the north may be seen the head of the great rift valley-system of Tithonius Lacus; the lofty, massive volcano Nodus Gordii lies off the photograph to the upper left. Photograph: 17 December 1971, from 6400 km.

2 Noctis Lacus The structure nicknamed 'The Chandelier': the picture covers an area of 542 × 246 km. Here we have a great system of canyons, each of which has an average width of 19 km — fully comparable with the Grand Canyon of the Colorado. This area marks the head of the great system of rift valleys lying to the east. Photographed on 9 January 1972, from an altitude of 8150 km.

3 Juventae Fons The picture covers an area of 350 × 450 km. Juventae Fons is one of the darkest areas on Mars. The direction of drainage is northward, along the boundary of Xanthe, but the track is much less well defined than that of the similar formation 1000 km to the west, where the drainage system is traceable as far as the Mare Acidalium. Photographed 31 January 1972.

4 Phoenicis Lacus Detail of the area at the intersection of the bottom two photographs of the mosaic picture. The fault valleys are clearly shown, while to the bottom of the picture there is still evidence of dust cover.

5 Sinuous Valley north of Argyre This remarkable valley is 400 km long, and 5 to 6 km broad in the section shown here. It has been compared with an 'arroyo', a watercut gully found in parts of the south-western United States; it lies about 300 km north of the boundary of the basin of Argyre. The drainage runs in a south-easterly direction. Photographed on 2 February 1972.

3

5

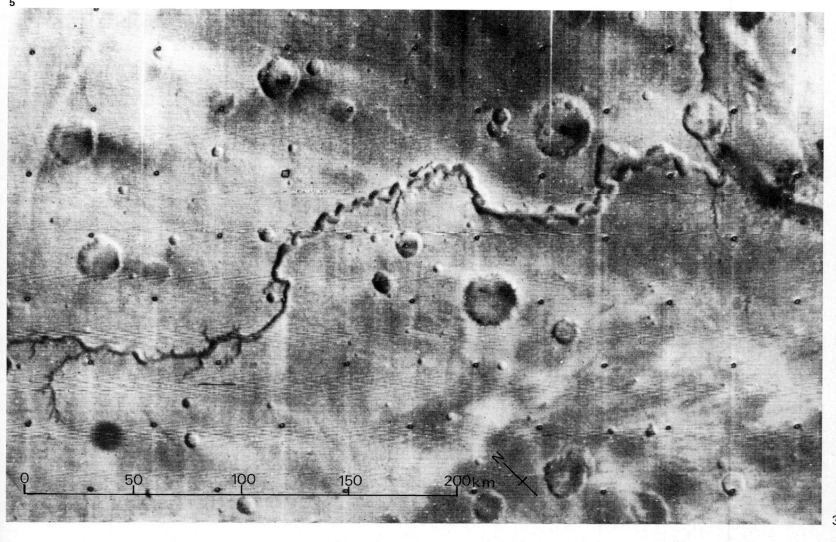

0   50   100   150   200km

THE SOUTH-EAST QUADRANT

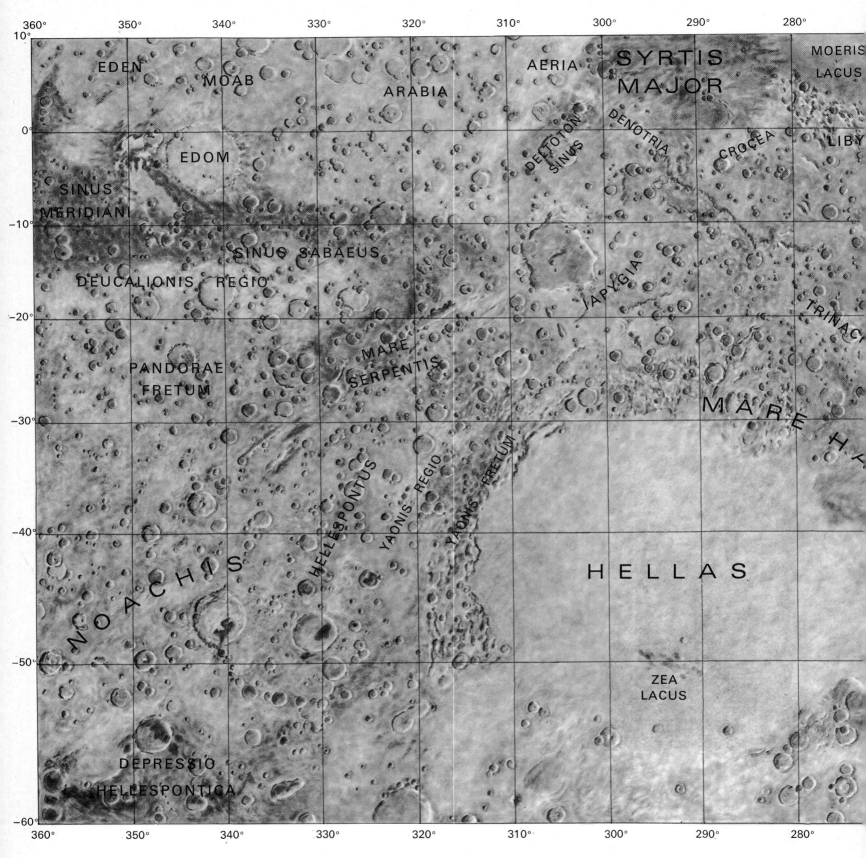

EDEN
MOAB
ARABIA
AERIA
SYRTIS MAJOR
MOERIS LACUS
EDOM
SINUS MERIDIANI
DELTOTON SINUS
DENOTRIA
CROCEA
LIBY
SINUS SABAEUS
DEUCALIONIS REGIO
JAPYGIA
TRINACI
PANDORAE FRETUM
MARE SERPENTIS
MARE H
HELLESPONTUS
YAONIS REGIO
YAONIS FRETUM
HELLAS
NOACHIS
ZEA LACUS
DEPRESSIO HELLESPONTICA

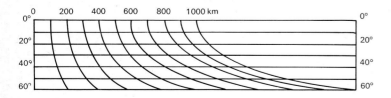

0   200   400   600   800   1000 km

Distances may be measured by using that
scale in the scale diagram which
corresponds to the latitude of the mid-point
of the measured distance.
Scale: 1:23,500,000 at the equator

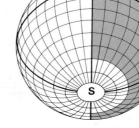

S

The coloured area on the globe indicates
the area referred to in the chart.

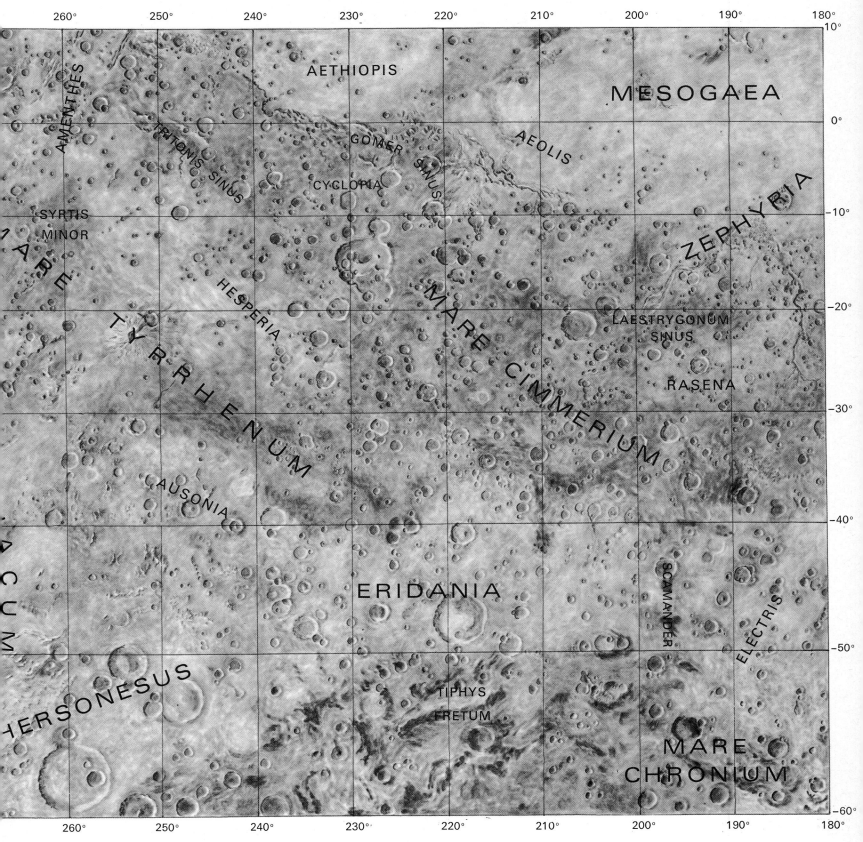

AETHIOPIS

MESOGAEA

AMENTHES

TRITONIS SINUS

GOMER SINUS

CYCLOPIA

AEOLIS

ZEPHYRIA

SYRTIS MINOR

MARE

HESPERIA

MARE CIMMERIUM

LAESTRYGONUM SINUS

RASENA

TYRRHENUM

AUSONIA

ERIDANIA

SCAMANDER

ELECTRIS

HERSONESUS

TIPHYS FRETUM

MARE CHRONIUM

This region of Mars is dominated by one remarkable feature: the circular plain Hellas. It is approximately 2000 km in diameter, and often appears very bright and white as seen from Earth. At times — as during the opposition of 1969 — it may be so prominent that it has been mistaken for an extra polar cap. Before the age of spacecraft Hellas was regarded as an elevated plateau, upon which white polar deposit persisted when the covering had disappeared from the adjacent areas. In fact, it is a depressed basin, and the lowest known feature upon the surface of Mars. Its basin lies 3 km below the 6·1 millibar level, and this is the only area on the planet where the atmospheric pressure is high enough for liquid water to exist today.

The most unusual characteristic of Hellas is that it shows virtually no interior detail. This paucity appears to be real, rather than being due to any low-lying obscuration over the floor. Nothing can be seen apart from one elusive feature which was noted by E. M. Antoniadi, and named by him Zea Lacus. His description of Hellas is historically interesting; he called it a large island or desert, comparable in area with our Greenland. He also commented that it is frequently covered by yellow clouds, particularly when Mars is near perihelion. In 1971 Hellas was much less conspicuous than during most preceding oppositions.

The western border of Hellas (Yaonis Fretum, Yaonis Regio) is better defined

than the eastern (Mare Hadriacum); this is probably because of the prevailing wind directions on Mars. West of Yaonis Fretum is the remarkable sand dune crater (seen on page 40), which again shows ripples in the material due to the influence of Martian winds. Hellas is not unique; Argyre I, in the southwestern quadrant, is of the same type, but undoubtedly Hellas is the best defined and the deepest of any such formations on Mars.

Well-defined volcanoes are rare in this quadrant, and the only two really good examples are to be found northeast of Hellas (approximate latitude −22°, longitude 253°). These volcanoes are unmistakable, but are much less massive and lofty than structures such as

Nix Olympica or Nodus Gordii. The region surrounding them is relatively free from craters, so that presumably the crater structures have been overlaid by volcanic ejecta. The bright area Hesperia may owe its relative lightness to such ejecta.

Much further to the east, in Rasena, there is a magnificent system of drainage valleys, and the drainage system can be traced along the boundaries of Zephyria and Aeolis. The slope of the ground is downward toward the north, so that the dark Mare Cimmerium is relatively high while the plains of Zephyria and Aeolis are much lower. At the very top of the map (approximate latitude −10°, longitude 290°) may be seen the southernmost extension of Syrtis Major

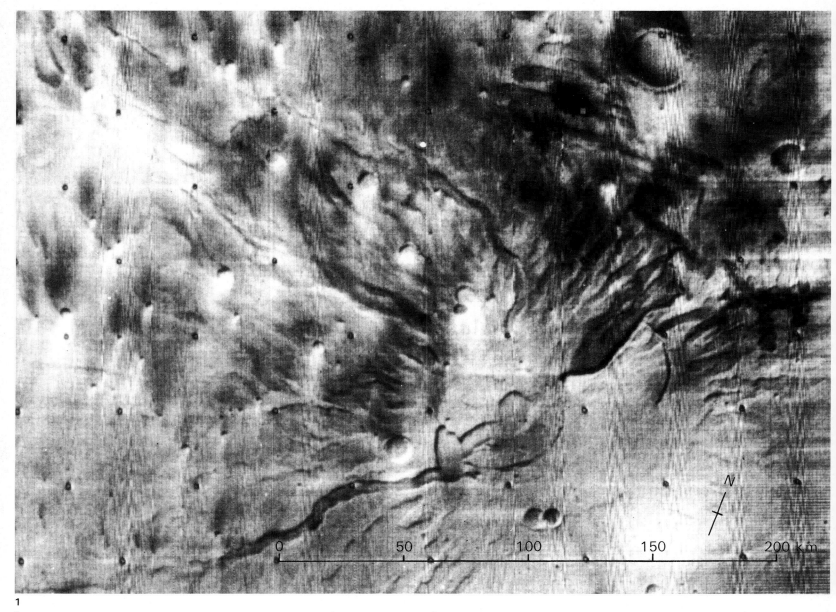

1

3

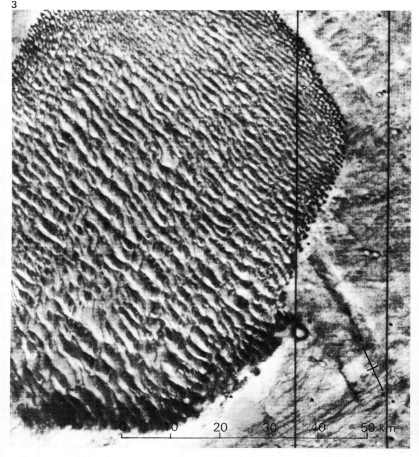

4

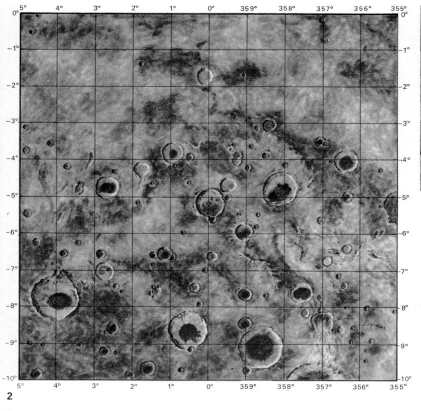

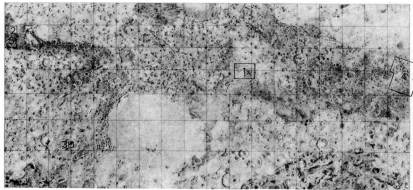

1 Volcanoes in Mare Tyrrhenum These are the best marked volcanoes in the quadrant. It seems that an old structure, with an 80 km crater on the crest of a volcano 140 km in base diameter, has been partially overlapped by a later eruption yielding a 40 km crater on a volcano of base diameter 180 km.

2 Airy-O Map of the area surrounding the crater Airy, seen in photograph 5. Airy-O is the tiny crater, almost in the centre of the main structure, which now marks the Martian zero longitude.

3 'Sand Dune' Crater in Hellespontus This is a remarkable feature, at latitude −48°, longitude 330°, on the cratered region of Hellespontus, which slopes down toward the Hellas basin. In the crater are what seem to be sand dunes. The exact nature of the material is uncertain; the prevailing wind direction is from the top right of the photograph.

4 Valley System in Rasena This is a complicated and extensive system of what may well be dried watercourses, between Zephyria and the Mare Cimmerium; the ground slopes downward toward the north (Zephyria), and the whole drainage system extends into Zephyria itself. Note how the valley cuts through two craters.

5 Airy In the Sinus Meridiani lies a crater now named Airy; the craterlet Airy-O, inside Airy itself, is now taken as the Martian zero for longitudes.

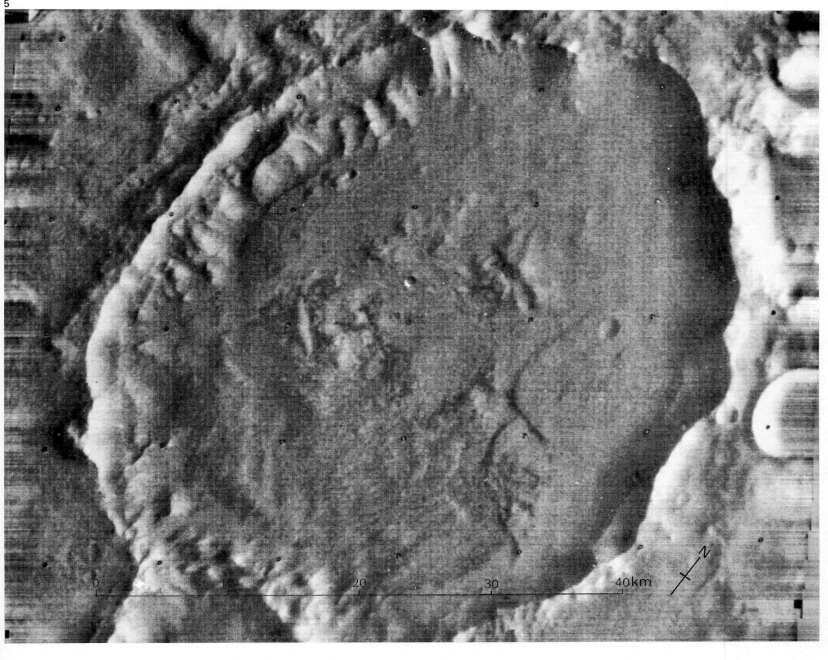

THE SOUTH POLE

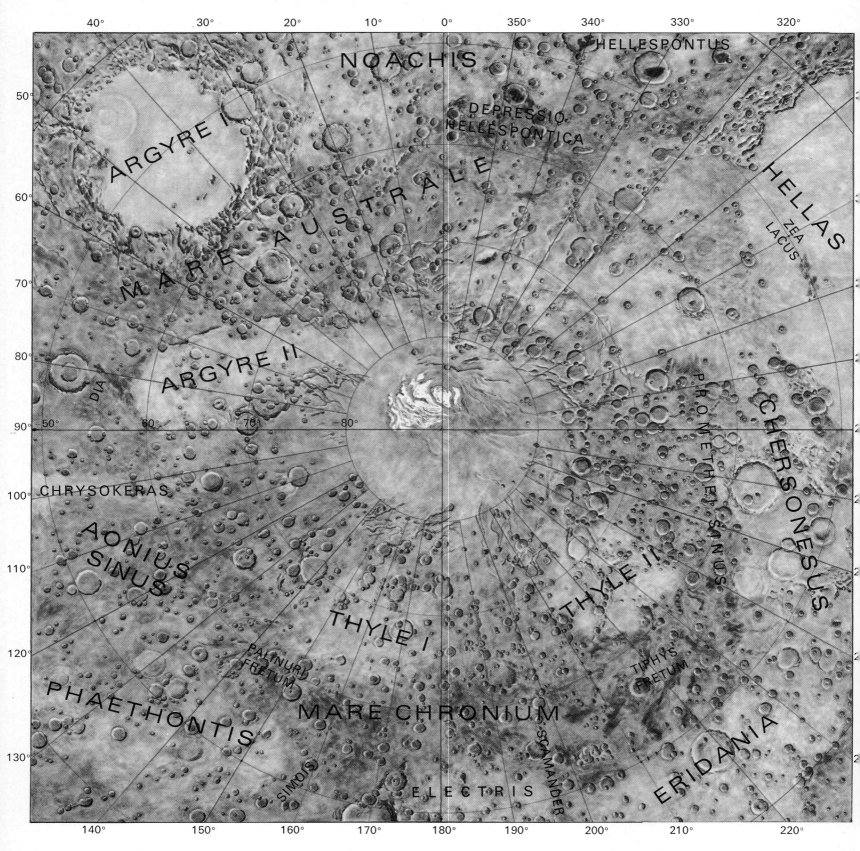

Map labels: 40°, 30°, 20°, 10°, 0°, 350°, 340°, 330°, 320°

NOACHIS — HELLESPONTUS — DEPRESSIO HELLESPONTICA — HELLAS — ZEA LACUS

ARGYRE I — MARE AUSTRALE

ARGYRE II — DIA — CHERSONESUS

CHRYSOKERAS — PROMETHEI SINUS

AONIUS SINUS — THYLE II

PHAETHONTIS — THYLE I — PALINURI FRETUM — MARE CHRONIUM — TIPHYS FRETUM — ERIDANIA

SIMOIS — SCAMANDER — ELECTRIS

Latitude labels: 50°, 60°, 70°, 80°, 90°, 100°, 110°, 120°, 130°

Bottom labels: 140°, 150°, 160°, 170°, 180°, 190°, 200°, 210°, 220°

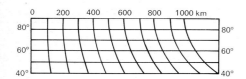

0 200 400 600 800 1000 km

Distances may be measured by using that scale in the scale diagram which corresponds to the latitude of the mid-point of the measured distance.
Scale: 1:23,500,000 at the equator

The coloured area on the globe indicates the area referred to in the chart.

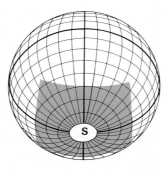

Summer in the southern hemisphere of Mars occurs when the planet is near perihelion, so the variations in size of the cap are greater than in the northern hemisphere because the melting effect of the Sun's rays is more extensive. At its greatest extent the cap may stretch down to past latitude −60°, whereas at minimum the cap has been known to disappear. The comparison of Mariner 7 and Mariner 9 results has emphasised this variation. The fly-past of Mariner 7 took place when the south cap was still very extensive, and vast areas of the polar zone were covered. Mariner 9 reached the neighbourhood of the planet, and entered orbit, much later in the Martian season, so that the whiteness was restricted to a small region. It is also

interesting to note that the cap is not centred on the geographical pole. As with the Earth, the coldest point does not lie exactly at the pole of rotation, but a short distance from it.

The area round the true pole shows few formations. This may well be because the old structures are covered by polar deposit, or have been eroded away. However, more detailed photographs will be needed before this particular problem can be solved.

Around latitude −60° there is a belt of darkish terrain extending more or less round the planet. This belt includes the Mare Australe and the Mare Chronium. During the Martian winter these areas are covered with polar deposit, as are Thyle I, Thyle II and Argyre II.

1

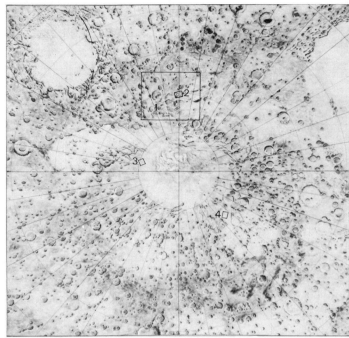

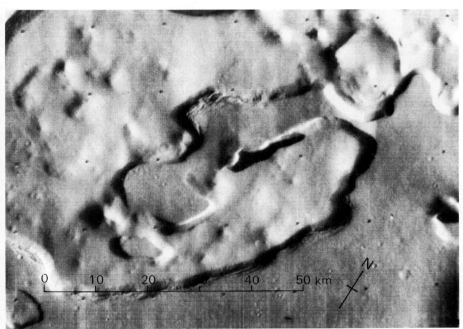

2

1 & 2 Pitted Plains Away from the pole there is an extensive transition region which is partly covered by smooth material like the laminated areas. There are however irregular pits in this layer which allow the rougher ground below to show through. Photograph 1, taken on 31 January, 1972, from 3500 km, shows a large area of this kind. Photograph 2, a telephoto picture taken 22 days later, shows the small marked area in close-up.

3 & 4 Laminated Terrain Telephoto pictures show that the polar cap and the surrounding smooth, crater-free terrain are built up of numerous superposed layers each of which is only 50 to 100 metres thick. Thus picture 3 shows an oval laminated plateau some 40×20 km, with a transition to pitted plains terrain along the northern edge of the picture. Picture 4 shows only laminated terrain.

4

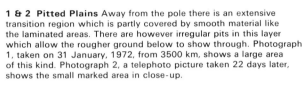
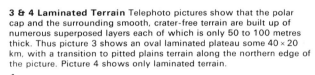

3

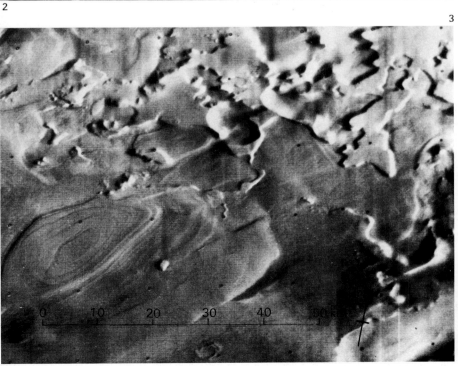

THE SATELLITES

For many years it was supposed that Mars, like Mercury and Venus, moved through space unattended by any satellites. Tennyson wrote a poem in which he referred to 'the snowy poles of moonless Mars'. In 1877, however, Asaph Hall, using the giant refractor at Washington, undertook a careful search, and detected two very small satellites, now known as Phobos and Deimos. Both are too faint to be seen without powerful equipment, even under the most favourable conditions of observation, and both are comparatively close to Mars. They are quite different in nature from our own massive Moon, and it is generally supposed that they are minor planets or asteroids which were captured by Mars in the remote past.

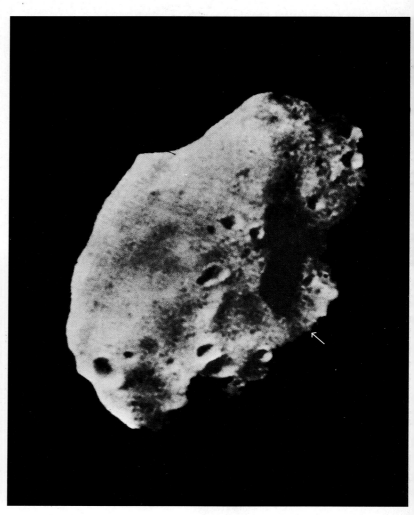

Both the Martian satellites are so small that from Earth they appear as tiny specks of light. Before the Mariner 9 photography we therefore knew nothing about their physical condition. The satellites show no measurable disks as seen from Earth, so estimates of their diameters originally depended upon assuming a mean albedo or reflecting power, and calculating the sizes simply from their apparent magnitudes. The values given by Antoniadi were 13 km for Phobos and 10 km for Deimos. It is now known that these estimates were rather too low, because the satellites have very feeble reflecting power; they are, in fact, the darkest objects known in the entire Solar System. Moreover, they are decidedly irregular in shape. This demonstrates the relative unimportance of gravity in controlling the shape of a small body; for Phobos and Deimos, the strength of the rock is sufficient to hold any configuration, whether spherical or not.

Phobos *below, right, far right* The apparent indentation towards the top on the first two pictures shows as a crater on the third. The south pole is marked with an arrow.

The first Photographs
The first close-range photographs of the satellites were obtained in 1969, and showed that Phobos is not spherical; it was then described as 'egg-shaped'. However, it was only with Mariner 9 that the first detailed photographs were obtained. Examination of the satellites was to some extent fortuitous, because the major dust storm meant that the surface of Mars could not be studied during the first weeks during which Mariner 9 was in orbit; although in fact the first photograph of Phobos had been obtained during the final approach of Mariner towards Mars, before a closed orbit round the planet had been achieved.

The first major discoveries were that both satellites are irregular in form, and that both have surfaces which are pitted with craters. The crater density is approximately the same as for the highlands of our Moon; for Phobos (much the better photographed of the two satellites) the largest formation has a diameter of $6\frac{1}{4}$ km. If these craters are due to impact, we must assume that all the debris arising from such collisions is lost into space; the escape velocities of the two satellites are negligible (20 kph and 10 kph respectively). The surfaces must have been eroded by the impacts of countless micro-meteorites, and by the solar wind. This presumably accounts for the unexpectedly low albedoes.

Not all the surfaces of the satellites could be photographed from Mariner 9 during the period of the spacecraft's active career, and maps of the surface features are therefore not yet complete; but the general configurations are ob-

Phobos *right* The approximate position of the south pole is indicated by an arrow. The south polar crater is again identifiable, and the crater near the top is the same as that which is coming into view in the first series. There is a pronounced surface bulge towards the top; this is the 'synchronous' bulge, permanently turned towards Mars.

vious enough. As had long been suspected (by Antoniadi and others) the satellites have captured or synchronous rotations, so that they always keep approximately the same faces turned towards Mars. The method of establishing this was by obtaining pictures of the satellites with the same angular relation between Mariner, Mars and the satellite concerned; the same features were always shown. There are, however, considerable diurnal librations in longitude: 42° for Phobos and 16° for Deimos (as against only 1° for the Moon as seen from Earth).

The Orbits of the Satellites
The orbits of both Martian satellites are less than 2° from the planet's equatorial plane and their polar axes are perpendicular to this plane. Also, the orbits are of very low eccentricity. This means that they pass across the Martian sky at a fixed zenith angle, depending on the observer's latitude, throughout the Martian year. They do not show appreciable optical librations, but their surfaces do experience the same seasonal variations in illumination as that of Mars itself.

The situation with the Earth's Moon is very different. The orbital plane is fairly close to that of the ecliptic, the polar axis is perpendicular to this plane, and the orbit is of appreciable eccentricity; therefore the Moon shows marked seasonal variations in zenith angle and appreciable optical libration in both latitude and longitude, but virtually no seasonal changes in surface illumination.

As seen from Mars, Phobos would rise in a westerly direction and set toward the east; it would remain above the horizon for only about $4\frac{1}{2}$ hours at a time, during which period it would go through more than half its cycle of phases. The interval between successive risings would be just over 11 hours. Deimos, whose period of revolution is only about six hours longer than the planet's rotation period, would remain above the horizon for two and a half Martian days successively.

Viewed from Mars
Neither would provide much illumination at night. From Mars, Phobos would have a maximum diameter of 12°·3, reducing to 7°·9 at rising or setting; this is less than half the apparent diameter of the Moon as seen from Earth. Deimos, smaller and more remote, would have an apparent diameter ranging between 2' and 1°·7, which is only about twice the maximum apparent diameter of Venus as seen from the Earth. The apparent magnitudes would be −3·9 and −0·1 respectively. In other words, Phobos would give about as much light as Venus sends to us, while the brightness of Deimos would be less than that of Sirius as seen from Earth. With the naked eye, the phases of Deimos would be almost imperceptible.

We must also remember that even when above the horizon, both satellites would spend long periods eclipsed by the shadow of Mars. Also, because the orbits are practically in the plane of the equator, neither satellite could be seen from high latitudes on Mars. Phobos would never rise as seen by an observer situated above latitude 69°; Deimos would never be seen by an observer standing above 82°.

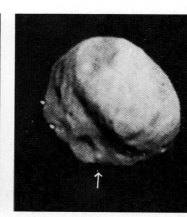

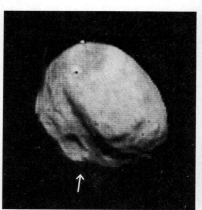

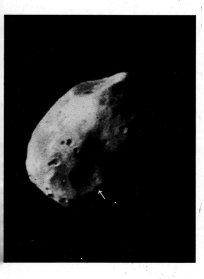

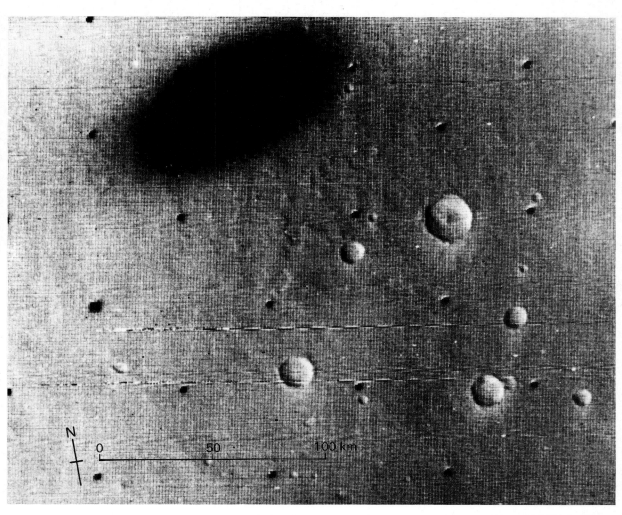

Eclipses

Total solar eclipses could never take place, because each satellite would appear much smaller than the Sun. Satellite transits would, however, be frequent. Phobos would transit 1300 times in each Martian year, taking approximately 19 seconds to pass right over the disk; Deimos would transit 130 times, with each transit taking about 1 minute 48 seconds. Of course, all these figures are subject to some variation to either side of the mean.

The nature of the satellites remains problematical. There can be no doubt that they are entirely different in character from our Moon, and from the major satellites of the giant planets; the theory that they are captured asteroids seems plausible, though it is true that some remarkable coincidence would be involved in view of the present orbits of the satellites. The idea that Phobos and Deimos might be used as space stations in the future is interesting, and cannot be entirely ruled out.

Shadow of Phobos on Mars *above* The photograph shows the region of Aethiopis, latitude +14°, longitude 235°; the group of craters can be identified on the map of the north-east quadrant of Mars (page 31). The shadow measures 50 by 109 km.

Satellite Data	Phobos	Deimos
Mean distance from centre of Mars:		
kilometres	9,270	23,400
astronomical units	0·0000625	0·0001570
Sidereal period: days	0·3189	1·2624
	(7h 39m)	(30h 18m)
Orbital eccentricity:	0·021	0·003
Orbital inclination (to Martian equator)	1·1°	1·8°
Diameter in kilometres:	22	12
Mean opposition magnitude:	11·6	12·8

Deimos *below* The photographs of Deimos are much fewer and less detailed than those of Phobos. One of the best *left* was obtained from a distance of 7781 km. The other photograph *right* shows merely an outline.

Comparison of Satellites *right* Phobos and Deimos as seen from Mars, and the Moon as seen from Earth. Only part of the Moon can be shown; Phobos and Deimos are given, to scale, as they would be seen from the Martian equator.

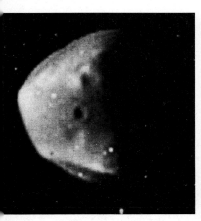

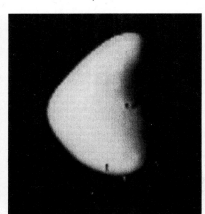

FUTURE EXPLORATION

The success of the Mariner probes of 1965 to 1972 has opened the way to the future exploration of Mars. It has already been shown that the soft-landing of a capsule is feasible; the Russians achieved it with Mars 3, and even though the capsule ceased to transmit after only twenty seconds the actual landing manoeuvre was carried through perfectly.

The next step in the American programme is to send up their Viking probe, which is scheduled to soft-land on Mars in 1976 — and should clear up, once and for all, the problem of whether there is or is not any life on Mars. It is still too early to say when the first manned expedition will go there. Everything depends upon whether the human body proves capable of enduring long periods of weightlessness. Yet if all is well, the 21st century should see the first man on Mars.

As with the 1969 and 1971 missions, the Viking programme will be undertaken with two identical spacecraft, to be launched within a few days of each other. The launching period will be August-September 1975, and the arrival on Mars will be in July-August 1976. When the landings take place, Mars will be almost 360,000,000 km from Earth, and on the other side of the Sun. From this distance a signal takes almost three quarters of an hour to travel from Earth to Mars and back, and so the entire descent manoeuvre must be completely automatic.

Each Viking spacecraft consists of an orbiter and lander. The initial launch from Cape Kennedy will put the probe into a 184 km 'parking orbit', and after a coast period of half an hour the Centaur — the upper portion of the launch vehicle — will re-ignite sending the spacecraft on its 360,000,000 km journey to Mars. During the journey the orbiter will supply electrical power, attitude control, and propulsion for any mid-course corrections, while the lander will be dormant.

The actual landing manoeuvre will be complicated. The situation is not the same as on the Moon, which is devoid of atmosphere. Parachute breaking is useful, though not sufficiently strong to be effective without rocket braking as well, and a heat shield is necessary.

The lander separates from the orbiter and entry into the Martian atmosphere will be made at about 26,000 metres above the planet's surface. The descent starts inside the aeroshell descent capsule, and at 6500 metres the main parachute opens. Then, at 1700 metres, the lander separates from the parachute, and completes the descent by means of its own engines. These engines will shut down about 13 metres from the surface, and the lander will fall gently onto the chosen landing site — which will be selected from those shown in the map above. Analysis of the Martian atmosphere will be made throughout the descent.

The Viking Orbiter
Viking is a complicated spacecraft. The orbiting section will remain in a closed path around Mars, with a rather eccentric orbit which carries it between 1500 km and 32,360 km from the planet in a period of 24·6 hours — one Martian day. It will send back information in the same way as the Mariners have done, but it will also act as a relay for the lander, and so it is a vital link in the whole chain of operations.

The main emphasis will be on the lander, and the success of the mission will be judged by the way in which the lander performs. The total weight of instruments carried to Mars cannot be great, so that immense care has gone into the selection of experiments to be carried — and all the equipment has to be made as light as possible. Inevitably, some interesting projects have had to be left out of the programme, but every possible use will be made of the space available.

Some investigations are fairly predictable. For instance, there will be a seismometer to measure any ground

tremors on Mars. The results of this experiment will be particularly interesting; Mars has giant volcanoes which were presumably active in the recent past (on the geological scale) and may conceivably be active now, in which case reasonably strong tremors cannot be ruled out. The seismometer should allow us to decide whether Mars is still tectonically energetic.

The atmosphere will be studied, this time from ground level, and reliable information about the velocities of Martian winds may be expected. We should also obtain a better analysis of the atmospheric composition, though it will be surprising if the results show anything but a preponderance of carbon dioxide. We should expect accurate temperature measurements, although we already know that the Martian climate is extremely cold.

Photographic Survey
Photographs of the area round the landing site should be clear, and, of course, the general scene will provide information about the Martian surface layer. Most fascinating of all will be the experi-

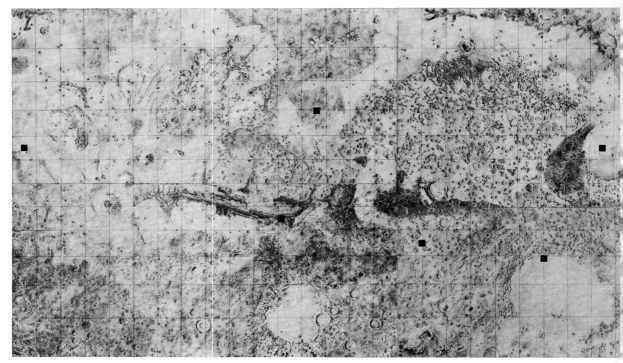

The Viking Landing Sites *above* The map shows the preliminary sites from which the final landing site for the Viking mission will probably be selected. The main zone of interest lies between latitude +30° and latitude −30°. Areas of high elevation are being avoided as far as possible.

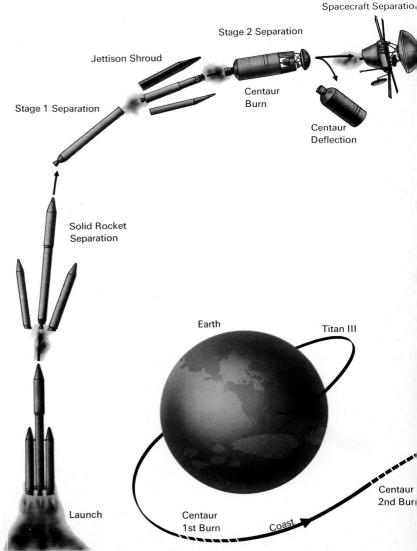

Viking Flight Sequence *right* The central portion of the diagram (not to scale) shows a contracted view of the stages of Viking's journey to Mars. The precise launch period was selected to provide a route to Mars which uses as little fuel as possible. The outer diagram gives a breakdown of the individual stages of the journey, the launch, the journey to Mars, the separation of the Lander and the descent, showing in detail the manoeuvres necessary for the landing of the Viking spacecraft.

Spacecraft Separation

Stage 2 Separation

Jettison Shroud

Centaur Burn

Stage 1 Separation

Centaur Deflection

Solid Rocket Separation

Earth

Titan III

Launch

Centaur 1st Burn

Coast

Centaur 2nd Burn

ments designed to detect any sign of life. Several of these are planned: one involves the scooping-up of some surface material for analysis in the spacecraft for organic material, while another will incubate the Martian material in a nutrient medium to detect the presence of living organisms.

The whole procedure is by far the most ambitious ever undertaken for a planetary probe. If it is carried through successfully, during the 1980s we may see automatic probes go to Mars and return with samples, although very efficient quarantining procedures will be essential before any Martian samples can be landed on Earth.

Nuclear spacecraft will presumably be developed before the end of the century, and it will be these which will in the end take the first pioneers to Mars.

Continuity of Exploration
The budget for Viking was approved even while Mariner 9 was still transmitting, and it is unlikely that exploration of Mars will stop there, even if the results are inconclusive or disappointing. We must also take Russian plans into account, although the Soviet authorities have not yet said much about what they propose to do.

In the early days of space research, the Russians experienced difficulty with long range communications. All their first planetary probes failed for this reason, and it was only in the late 1960s that they overcame their difficulties. Mars 2 and Mars 3 of 1971–2 were their first successes with Mars, and even these were only partial. It is reasonable

Viking: Exploded View *right* Each spacecraft consists of an Orbiter and a Lander, which will make the soft landing on Mars. In the diagram the Orbiter is shown at the bottom. The Lander is protected against the heat of the journey through the Martian atmosphere in a capsule formed by the bioshield's cap and base.

to believe that a Soviet lander will reach Mars at about the same time as the Viking, and that its programme of research will be very much the same. The landing procedure for the Mars 3 capsule certainly involved the same procedure as the plans that have been published for Viking.

Russian emphasis
The Russians are placing more and more emphasis on purely automatic probes. Their Lunokhod vehicle, which crawled around the Moon for almost the whole of 1970, was a great triumph, and it may well be that they plan something similar for Mars, though the problems are very much greater. In any case, it seems that the Russians, as well as the Americans, are deeply interested in the Red Planet, and that they will not relax in their efforts to find out more about its surface, its structure, its history and its many other mysteries.

Viking Lander *below right* The Lander vehicle contains equipment for photographic work and experiments in biology, molecular analysis of the soil, atmosphere composition, meteorology, earthquakes and the magnetic and physical properties of the planet. The diagram shows the layout of the visible equipment.

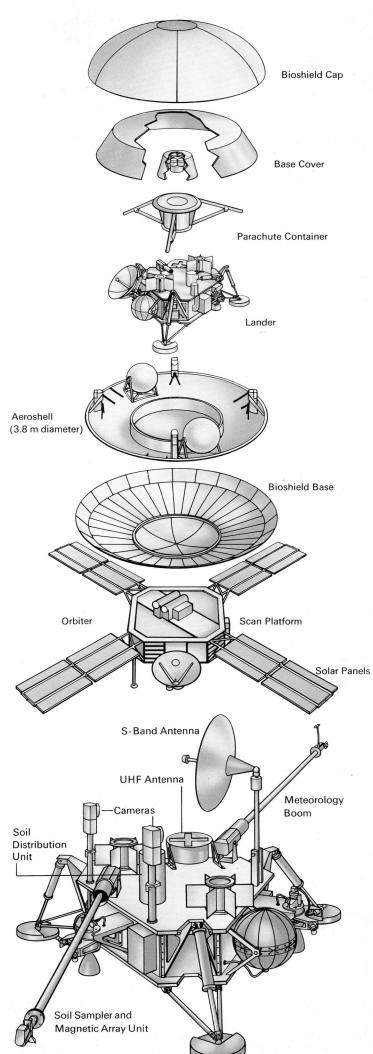

Bioshield Cap

Base Cover

Parachute Container

Lander

Aeroshell (3.8 m diameter)

Bioshield Base

Orbiter

Scan Platform

Solar Panels

S-Band Antenna

UHF Antenna

Cameras

Soil Distribution Unit

Meteorology Boom

Soil Sampler and Magnetic Array Unit

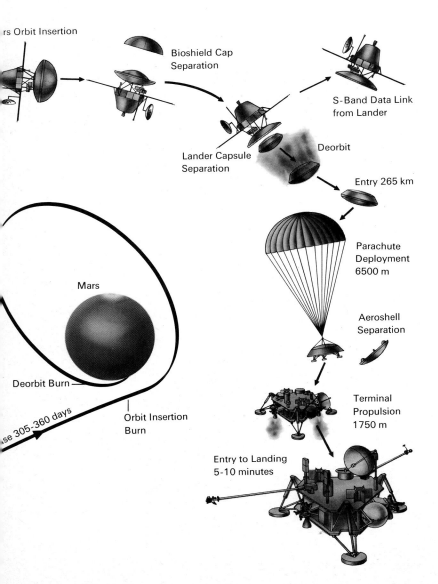

rs Orbit Insertion

Bioshield Cap Separation

S-Band Data Link from Lander

Lander Capsule Separation

Deorbit

Entry 265 km

Parachute Deployment 6500 m

Aeroshell Separation

Terminal Propulsion 1750 m

Entry to Landing 5-10 minutes

Mars

Deorbit Burn

se 305-360 days

Orbit Insertion Burn

INDEX

Photographic acknowledgments

C. F. Capen, 7, 9, 12(1–4)
W. S. Finsen, 12(5,6)
Patrick Moore's collection, 5, 13, 14(Mariner 9), 16, 18(Crater
   Lake, Tsiolkovskii)
NASA, 8, 15(Mariner 4, Mariner 9), 17, 18(Martian crater,
   CO$_2$ trace), 19, 20, 22, 23, 25, 28, 29, 32, 33, 36, 37, 40, 41,
   43, 44, 45.
Novosti, 14(Mars 1), 15(Mars 3)